"A must read for clinicians facing the challenge of treating borderline personality disorder. The book provides practical, wise, and immediately helpful advice that will improve your next session."

> —*Allen Frances, MD, professor and chair of the Department of Psychiatry and Behavioral Sciences at the Duke University Medical Center and chair of the Task Force on the DSM-IV*

"Preston had taken on a Herculean task. First, he has written a book on the treatment of individuals with borderline personality disorder, and second, he has offered a protocol for the shorter-term treatments of these individuals. He had succeeded brilliantly in both areas. From conceptualization through diagnosis and treatment, this volume offers both experienced and novice clinicians a practical, applied, and straightforward framework for increasing the potential for therapeutic success with this most difficult and diverse client group."

> —*Arthur Freeman, Ed.D., ABPP, professor and chair of the Department of Psychology at the Philadelphia College of Osteopathic Medicine*

Integrative Treatment *for* Borderline Personality Disorder

Effective, Symptom-Focused Techniques, Simplified for Private Practice

JOHN D. PRESTON, PSY.D., ABPP

New Harbinger Publications, Inc.

Publisher's Note

This publication is designed to provide accurate and authoritative information in regard to the subject matter covered. It is sold with the understanding that the publisher is not engaged in rendering psychological, financial, legal, or other professional services. If expert assistance or counseling is needed, the services of a competent professional should be sought.

Distributed in Canada by Raincoast Books

Copyright © 2006 by John D. Preston, Psy.D.
New Harbinger Publications, Inc.
5674 Shattuck Avenue
Oakland, CA 94609

Cover design by Amy Shoup; Acquired by Melissa Kirk; Text design by Tracy Marie Carlson

Library of Congress Cataloging-in-Publication Data

Preston, John, 1950-
   Integrative treatment for borderline personality disorder : effective, symptom-focused techniques, simplified for independent practice / John D. Preston.
      p. ; cm.
   Includes bibliographical references and index.
   ISBN-13: 978-1-57224-446-7
   ISBN-10: 1-57224-446-1
   1. Borderline personality disorder—Treatment. 2. Brief psychotherapy. I. Title.
   [DNLM: 1. Borderline Personality Disorder—therapy. 2. Psychotherapy, Brief—methods. WM 190 P938i 2006]
   RC569.5.B67P756 2006
   616.85'85206—dc22

                                    2005037412

FSC
Mixed Sources
Product group from well-managed
forests and other controlled sources
Cert no. SW-COC-002283
www.fsc.org
© 1996 Forest Stewardship Council

RAINFOREST ALLIANCE
CERTIFIED

All Rights Reserved
Printed in the United States of America
New Harbinger Publications' website address: www.newharbinger.com

13   12   11

10   9   8   7   6

Dedicated, with appreciation, to

Marsha Linehan

These clients "... never benefit from being told that they are narcissistic or borderline. These labels which have done so much aid [research] ... now serve more to protect us from our own feelings of incompetence, to ward off or reduce the dysphoria experienced by us therapists when patients seem to get worse in the face of our best efforts."

—Donald L. Nathanson, M.D.,
author of *Shame and Pride*

Contents

PART III
TREATMENT ISSUES

PART IV
TREATMENT STRATEGIES

Many thanks to the staff of New Harbinger Publications. As usual you have been most helpful. I also want to gratefully acknowledge the guidance of my publisher Dr. Matthew McKay and superb editing from Kayla Sussell. Your suggestions and encouragement have meant a lot to me.

I owe so much to the lessons I have learned from my clients during my 30 years of clinical practice. You have helped me to know more about suffering, surviving, and personal courage.

Finally, I want to thank my soul-mate and best friend, Bonnie Preston. Bonnie is also a psychologist. Together we have tried to learn how to face the human suffering inherent in this work, we have struggled to maintain hope even when things seemed hopeless, and have discovered some ways to help our clients to heal. This is your book too, Bonnie.

Special thanks to my colleagues and friends, Drs. John O'Neal, and Marty Johnson.

INTRODUCTION

The Challenge

All psychotherapists encounter clients who are difficult to treat, clients who push us to the limits of our skills and often our own emotional tolerance. Most therapists will agree that people with severe personality disorders top the list of tough patients. It is frustrating and at times painful to treat these clients, in part because we have to witness their intense and prolonged suffering. It is also difficult because, owing to the nature of their psychopathology, they can really get to us. Probably more than any other group of mental health clients, people with severe personality disorders evoke and provoke strong reactions in others. It is hard to imagine that any therapist hasn't had times of feeling overwhelmed, frustrated, impatient, and angry in the course of treating these patients.

In addition, another common feeling that therapists often experience when working with borderline clients is that of impotence. Often, as we bring to bear our most well-developed skills and honest efforts to be empathic and helpful, we crash on the rocks of therapeutic stalemate. Some "experts" may say that they have mastered the ability to treat borderline patients, but let's be honest . . . all therapists, even the most competent, struggle a lot with these challenging clients. That is the rule, not the exception!

The difficulties in treating borderline patients are further amplified in the context of today's managed care environment in which most therapists must provide only brief therapy. Short-term psychotherapy has evolved in response to two major forces. The first, of course, is cost containment. The second is the desire to reduce human emotional suffering as quickly as possible. This second motivation was a key factor influencing the early pioneers of the brief therapy movement, and I would hope that it continues to be recognized as a legitimate factor in the provision of short-term treatment.

The majority of books and articles written addressing shorter-term therapy, however, focus on treatment approaches suited for relatively high-level functioning clients (e.g., people experiencing acute adjustment disorders and neurotic-level pathology). And, clearly, brief treatment can and does help many people. It has also made psychotherapy available to many thousands of people who, in previous years, would not have had access to psychological treatments. However, little attention has been paid to shorter-term treatments for borderline personality disorders (BPD).

The now rather voluminous literature addressing psychological and psychiatric treatments of BPD almost exclusively recommends lengthy treatment (either two or three times per week, or once-a-week therapy that extends for a number of years). One notable exception is the work of Marsha Linehan and colleagues who have developed *dialectical behavior therapy* or DBT (Linehan, 1993 a; 1993 b). This treatment is typically offered on a once-a-week basis (one session of individual and one session of group therapy), typically extending for a period of twelve to eighteen months. The focus on longer-term treatment is certainly influenced by the theoretical models endorsed by leading experts in this area, many of whom espouse psychodynamic theories. It is likely that longer-term, intensive psychotherapy is also recommended because of the nature of the disorder itself (severe, pervasive, and chronic psychopathology). However, it is important to note the results from a meta-analysis of psychotherapy studies conducted by Perry (1999). In this article, fifteen outcome studies that represent the treatment of 800 borderline patients are reviewed. The mean number of sessions was only forty, and each study yielded positive outcomes. The approaches included in this meta-analysis varied from psychodynamic therapy (N: 9 studies) to cognitive behavioral (N: 6). The average number of sessions may more closely approximate what is done in the real world. And, these positive results appear to challenge the assumption that long-term, intensive treatment is essential for good outcomes with borderline clients.

As I see it, here is the problem: Long-term psychotherapy may be beneficial or even necessary for some people with a diagnosis of BPD. However, I suspect that only a tiny percentage of borderline patients can afford such treatment. Insurance companies, as we all know, have increasingly restricted benefits and some HMOs have developed policies that actually exclude or disallow psychiatric treatment to those deemed to be a "poor brief therapy candidate." Borderline patients are often so dysfunctional that they do not have the ability to earn a good income and/or they experience significant occupational instability.

The bottom line is this: These people who suffer so much cannot afford long-term treatment. And therapists who take on BPD clients are often at a loss about how to treat them when shorter-term therapy is mandated by third-party payers or limited financial resources. That is the dilemma.

So, what often happens is that therapists either refuse to treat people with severe personality disorders or they take them on and do their best. I've worked in clinics and hospitals where I observed what I believe to be a common phenomenon. Therapists develop a judgmental, almost disparaging attitude towards clients with BPD, which is reflected by frequent statements such as, "Oh, God, not another borderline," or "She's a flaming borderline." Most people with a diagnosis of BPD have a terrible history of experiencing abuse, neglect, humiliation, and rejection in their families of origin. And then they enter health care systems only to encounter additional interpersonal interactions that often communicate (at least covertly) a degrading, rejecting message.

It is not my intention to point a critical finger at therapists, for I believe that the negative attitude I have described is most often a defense against feelings of impotence. Most therapists want to be helpful. We entered this field hoping to make a difference in the lives of fellow human beings. We are also like anyone else in our desire to feel competent and successful. In addition to the multitude of feelings and countertransference reactions provoked by BPD clients (as will be discussed in greater detail), there is also the often difficult task of trying to help these people when constrained by the fact that only brief therapy can be provided. Let's be realistic, these are very challenging patients and it is a very tall order to work with them when you are restricted in the number of sessions you can provide. I certainly have been tremendously frustrated when I believed a client needed a lot more therapy (in terms of the number of sessions) and then we both ran into the reality of limited benefits.

One response to these constraints can be to blame the victim and feel critical towards our client. Another possible response is to develop a pervasive sense of therapeutic nihilism (which often leads to an increasing sense of bitterness or burnout). You know it and I know it . . . this happens. Another possible response is what I address in this book—to adopt a three-pronged perspective on this issue.

The first prong is a humbling but very important acknowledgment of our limitations as treaters and healers. It's crucial to know what we are up against in taking on these challenging cases. It's called severe, entrenched psychopathology. For reasons that are unclear to me, psychotherapy has been dominated by the goal of "curing" mental illness. I believe that this reflects a great deal of naiveté. Some human problems are caused by hard-wired neurobiological conditions or reflect deeply ingrained character pathology, both of which may be helped with treatment, but which are also very likely to continue as part of the fabric of human personalities. Realistically acknowledging our limitations is not, however, admitting defeat. Rather, it is possible to see therapy aimed not so much at "curing" but at "facilitating change." With many BPD clients we can do a great deal to help them cope more successfully and suffer less—even with shorter-term treatment. This is an important and honorable thing to do.

The second prong or element is developing and honing our skills as therapists. Owing to the complexity of borderline disorders and the challenges in treating these clients, I will argue that it makes sense to employ integrative approaches to treatment (i.e., using both empirically validated psychological therapies and treatments that target neurobiology, including pharmacotherapy). No single theoretical model can fully explain borderline pathology, and integrative treatment strategies may give us our best shot at helping these clients. The approaches recommended in this book will adopt a somewhat shorter-term format of individual, once-a-week psychotherapy that is designed to last from 4-18 months.

The third prong is the therapist's role in influencing health care policy making. As a group of professionals, we have the opportunity to speak out regarding decisions that affect access to mental health services. In medicine it is recognized that there are some disorders that require more intensive care or even necessitate life-long therapies (e.g., hypertension and diabetes), and there are certain diseases that can be adequately addressed by way of time-limited outpatient treatment. Similarly, I suggest that we can offer much to borderline patients in shorter-term treatment. As radical as this might sound, sometimes brief treatment is even the treatment of choice. However, it is also clear that some people require lengthier therapy, and failure to provide this will result in continuing emotional suffering that sometimes will culminate in suicide (approximately 10 percent of borderline patients ultimately kill themselves). Beyond the suffering of the identified patient, the adverse impact of borderline pathology on the ability to parent is enormous. Failure to aggressively treat BPD in those who have children can result in significantly traumatic experiences for their children, and in fact, such experiences of abuse or neglect may contribute to what can be seen as a form or inter-generational transmission of psychopathology. Often borderline parents beget borderline offspring. While we are developing and refining techniques to carry out more successful treatment, we can also take a stand for what is right and bring pressures to bear on those making the decisions that affect insurance and mental health care benefits. In the words of Dr. Martin Luther King, Jr., "Our lives begin to end when we become silent about things that matter."

VALUING OUR TREATMENT

One editorial comment before you dive into the material. Some experts have implied that "real" psychotherapy for the treatment of severe personality disorders must be lengthy (carried on for years) and frequent (two to three times per week). They hold that anything less than this intensive, long-term treatment is not real therapy, but rather, is "counseling," as they refer to it. The implication is that shorter-term approaches are somehow second-rate.

I want to be clear; in my view, a once-a week and relatively time-limited approach to treatment for BPD absolutely is psychotherapy. And, furthermore, it is some of the most difficult, challenging treatment that psychotherapists can undertake. To help borderline clients, especially under the constraints of time-limited treatment, requires considerable skill and experience. Additionally, riding out affective storms, containing countertransference reactions, and maintaining emotional availability demands significant psychological maturity and sturdiness on the part of therapists.

I have attempted to write a book that is practical, applied, and straightforward. Like most therapists, I am influenced by theoretical models, and this will be apparent in the chapters that follow. At the same time, I have tried to write a book that focuses primarily on the nuts and bolts of diagnosis and treatment strategies and incorporates approaches from a number of different theoretical frames of reference. It is my sincere hope you will find this material useful in your clinical work.

So, let's get started.

PART I

BASIC DIAGNOSTIC ISSUES

CHAPTER 1

Diagnosis

A BRIEF HISTORY OF THE DIAGNOSIS OF THE DISORDER

In the late 1940s and early '50s the first articles were written describing a perplexing group of psychotherapy patients. These people often looked healthy—at least superficially. Early in treatment they were often seen as neurotics. Yet, as psychotherapy got under way, unexpected behaviors emerged; e.g., severe regressions, explosive emotions, self-mutilation, psychosis . . . clearly, not what is seen in garden-variety neurotics. These patients were not only bewildering, they were also a source of considerable stress for the therapists who treated them. They developed intense hostile and/or dependent transferences (Waldinger and Gunderson 1987) and tested the endurance of even very seasoned therapists.

Early clinicians and writers described these clients by various names, "pseudo-neurotic schizophrenia" (Hoch and Polatin 1949), "borderline states" (Knight 1953), borderline schizophrenia, and ultimately, borderline personality disorder.

The time was ripe for proponents of various theoretical schools to jump at this newly diagnosed disorder and begin weaving it into the structure of existing models. A disorder that somehow straddled the line between neurosis and psychosis conveniently met the needs of those psychoanalytic writers who liked to conceive of mental health as existing on a continuum—extending from severe psychosis on one end to emotional health on the other. In a sense, borderline disorders could be seen as the "missing link" between psychosis and neurosis.

Prevalence of Severe Personality Disorders in the General Population

Disorder	Prevalence Rate
Borderline	1.8–4 percent
Antisocial	1–3 percent
Schizotypal	3 percent
Paranoid	0.5–2.5 percent
Narcissistic	1 percent

Sources: APA 1994; Gabbard 1996

Familial Pattern: BPD

- Borderline personality disorder is approximately five times more common among first-degree biological relatives than in the general population.

Source: DSM IV, APA 1994, p. 653

A different view was entertained by the more biologically oriented theorists who had begun to note that relatives of schizophrenics often did not exhibit frank psychotic disorders, but did manifest patterns of peculiar thinking and odd behavior (what, these days we would classify as variants of schizophrenic-spectrum disorders, such as schizotypal personality disorder).

As Waldinger and Gunderson noted (1987, p. 7), although many different views regarding etiology have been posited, in many respects most theoreticians have come to fairly similar conclusions regarding treatment approaches. All agree that these patients are exceptionally difficult to treat and that they have an almost uncanny ability to provoke strong countertransference reactions in therapists. Most theoreticians are also in agreement about some of the fundamental guidelines to observe in treating this group of patients.

Not All Borderlines Are Alike

Although many authors write about borderline personality disorder (possibly implying a single entity) the evidence is abundant that what exists is a tremendously heterogeneous group of disorders. In 1968, Grinker et al. did the first empirical study of clients with severe personality disorders. The authors conducted a cluster analysis based on a checklist of ninety-three different markers of ego functioning. Rather than isolating one group, the data showed four somewhat distinct clusters (or subtypes). These are described below.

The Four Subtypes of Borderline Personality Disorder

1. Borderline patients who are prone to transient psychotic episodes. These people also exhibited more impairments in thinking than did the other groups (e.g., paranoid ideations, ideas of reference, idiosyncratic reasoning).

2. "Core Borderlines" present a history of very unstable interpersonal relationships, a tendency to experience depression, and are especially characterized by intense anger (along with irritability, volatility, and impulsivity). These patients also displayed a good deal of destructive acting out behavior. Despite their chaotic lives and affective dyscontrol, these borderline people (unlike group No. 1) rarely become psychotic.

3. Borderline patients with a dominant presentation of affective blandness and emptiness. These people appeared to have a grossly underdeveloped sense of self (a group referred to as "as if" personalities by Deutsch in 1944).

4. The final group was characterized as severely dysthymic, clingy, emotionally reactive, and highly egocentric individuals. These people are interpersonally very needy and prone to experience significant emotional despair if they encounter rejections or losses (even minor social rebuffs or criticisms). This group closely fits the description of "hysteroid-dysphoria" (Klein 1969).

Too often in the history of psychiatry a critical mistake is made where quite heterogeneous groups of patients are lumped together into broad categories and treated as if they were a homogeneous group. This methodological flaw can seriously derail research on diagnosis and treatment. Suffice it to say, Grinker and his colleagues made an important contribution in 1968 when they launched the search for relevant subtypes of severe personality disorders.

Ego Functioning and the Concept of Borderline "Level"

In the late 1960s and early 1970s Kernberg shifted the focus away from specific behaviors and symptoms to a consideration of intrapsychic characteristics. In addition to his development of an etiologic hypothesis, Kernberg introduced the concept of "borderline *level* of personality organization" (1967). Rather than viewing borderline personality disorder as a personality *type* or a specific diagnosis, he presented the idea that there is a spectrum of disorders that can be understood as functioning at a borderline *level* with regard to ego functioning. Although there may be many different styles of personality (e.g., obsessional, histrionic, paranoid, etc.), the one thing they share in common is weak ego functioning (i.e., overall adaptive functioning that is more impaired than that which is seen in neurotics, but more intact than that seen in patients with psychotic disorders).

The Ego Functions Model

The ego has been referred to as the "organ of adaptation." According to psychodynamic thinking, people are born with a set of "ego potentials." (In this context, "psychodynamic" refers broadly to models influenced by psychoanalytic theory including psychoanalysis, ego psychology, object relations theory, and self-psychology.) With the provision of adequate physical needs, with "good enough" parenting, an intact central nervous system, and good luck (fate), the child progressively matures. An important aspect of the child's developmental progress is the emergence of certain adaptive skills and capabilities, personal affective and cognitive abilities that enable the child to accomplish three parallel goals:

1. To survive,

2. To adapt to the demands of the social/interpersonal world, and

Key Characteristics of Severe Personality Disorders

- **Dependent/Histrionic BPD**: Extreme sensitivity to actual or imagined interpersonal rejection/abandonment

- **Paranoid**: All are suspicious and mistrusting

  Two subtypes are seen clinically:

  The aggressive paranoid: Chip on the shoulder, quick to anger, strongly motivated to avoid feeling powerless

  The fearful paranoid: Feels very vulnerable; afraid of being controlled or physically injured

- **Narcissistic**: Cockiness, and grandiosity mask significant feelings of shame, humiliation, and low self-esteem

- **Schizoid or Schizotypal**: Very socially isolated (egosyntonic); needs a lot of alone time, anxious when forced to interact with others (outside of immediate family)

- **Obsessional BPD**: Attempts to control and contain emotional expression; brittle rigidity. Significantly distressed by affect arousal and unpredictability

- **Antisocial/Psychopath**: Derives gratification by using or hurting others. Strongly motivated to avoid situations provoking feelings of powerless

3. To gradually develop a unique "self."

This set of skills and capabilities has been described by many as *ego functions*. The ego functions model is an important conceptual template that we will discuss in greater detail in the next section, "Diagnostic Issues: Ego Strength."

For Kernberg, and many other theorists/clinicians, the defining hallmark of borderline level pathology can be stated rather simply:

- It represents a persistent disorder that often first develops in late childhood or, at least, by early adulthood. It is not just a symptom disorder that emerges in the wake of significant stressors. Rather, it is a pervasive problem, an often life-long state of vulnerability that results in what some have called "stable instability" (i.e., marked by a *long* history of affective and interpersonal instability).

- It is recognizable by significant signs of ego weakness (e.g., inadequate affective controls, volatility, impulsivity, exquisite emotional sensitivity, impaired thinking and other signs of ego impairment), but with an *absence of sustained* psychotic symptomology (Kernberg 1975).

DSM-IV and Beyond

Although the DSM-IV has provided a number of diagnostic criteria (allowing for a rather large array of possible symptomatic combinations and thus various types of borderline diagnoses), in many respects the DSM borderline personality disorder criteria are biased towards the description of a rather histrionic, dependent, affective-disordered borderline diagnosis (Kroll 1988). Stone (1980) and others have argued, and I agree, that there are numerous variations on this borderline theme—all sorts of shades and styles.

Thus, for example, a group of patients may be described as "obsessional personalities" who are characterized by such traits as emotional constriction and rigidity, a lack of humor, excessive devotion to work, a tendency to overintellectualize, and "anal-retentive" behaviors. Some of these obsessional personalities (despite their problems and limitations) exhibit a high level of ego functioning and may be seen as neurotic (or sometimes as healthier than neurotic). Others, however, with the same *characterological style*, may show signs of ego weakness. Their cognitive style, preferences for intellectual pursuits, and emotional rigidity traits appear to be similar to the obsessional neurotic, but what bleeds through are signs of impaired ego functioning (i.e., occasional magical thinking or urges to self-mutilate).

What is implied here is a two-dimensional matrix for understanding personality disorders. One axis accounts for the variety of personality "styles," while the other addresses the level of ego functioning. (See Figure 1.1).

As our understanding of borderline disorders has grown and evolved since the late 1940s, it has become clear that there are many different types of people who may be aptly described as borderline. It is important to make distinctions among subtypes, especially for research purposes, while also understanding that all borderline level clients do share some common core symptoms, liabilities, and vulnerabilities. (See Chapter 3.) As Figure 1.1 implies, the first important question to ask is "What *kind* of person am I working with?" (i.e., what's his or her "style") *and* then to ask, "What is his or her overall level of functioning?" These are not just academic questions; they are the questions that lead us to specific treatment strategies and precautions.

Let's expand this issue of "level of functioning" by taking a closer look at some diagnostic issues.

DIAGNOSTIC ISSUES: EGO STRENGTH

> "[I]n embarking on therapy with a particular patient, the journey will be greatly facilitated if the therapist makes use of a map . . . as every psycho-therapist can testify, there is recurrent danger of getting lost." (Strupp and Binder 1984, p.xvii)

Diagnosis is a continually *ongoing* process of understanding the client. However, it is especially important for the therapist to have a clear picture of the client's level of functioning early in treatment, particularly if the goal is to provide brief therapy (defined in this book generally as weekly therapy sessions for one to one-and-a-half years). Understanding the level of functioning is crucial for establishing realistic thera-peutic goals, avoiding catastrophes, and providing limit setting—starting with the very first session.

In this section we will look at several diagnostic perspectives that are helpful both for assessing the client in the opening sessions and as a way to monitor behavioral changes while treatment proceeds. Hopefully, these diagnostic issues will help you to construct a "map" that will inform your treatment interventions at each step along the way.

Personality Styles	Continuum: High functioning, emotionally mature	Neurotic level	Borderline level	Psychotic level
Shy, detached				
Shy, dependent				
Gregarious, dependent, histrionic				
Rigid, constricted, obsessional				
Suspicious, paranoid (1)				
Antisocial (1)				
Narcissistic				
Mixed				

Level of Ego Functioning

1. Well-functioning versions of this style probably do not exist.

Figure 1.1. Personality Styles

EGO FUNCTIONS

As mentioned in the last section, many clinicians have viewed borderline pathology as primarily involving inadequate ego functions. This notion is an outgrowth of psychoanalytic theory, but, in my view, it is a perspective that is acceptable to many therapists: even those disinclined to think in psychodynamic terms. The model was developed and refined by Bellack and colleagues (1973).

> The prevalence of borderline personality disorder is somewhere between 1.8 percent and 4 percent of the general population. BPD patients represent 11 percent and 23 percent of clients seen in outpatient and inpatient mental health settings, respectively (Gabbard 1996b). The 20:80 rule probably is worth noting: 20 percent of our toughest clients take 80 percent of our time, energy, and emotional resources. Borderline patients make up a big part of this 20 percent.

Resistance to Dysfunction

Let's begin this section with a brief discussion of the concept of *ego strength*. In general terms, ego strength refers to the degree of emotional durability and adaptability a person exhibits (especially in the face of significant psychosocial stressors). It is best understood in terms of *resistance to dysfunction* and *resiliency*. Resistance to dysfunction implies that even when confronted with serious stressors, the person with well-developed ego strength continues to function and does not emotionally collapse. This is not to suggest that such people do not experience emotional suffering. Quite the contrary. People with strong egos absolutely do experience and express a full range of human emotions during crises. In fact, their ability to appropriately experience and express feelings (e.g., sadness, anger, joy, and so forth) is one sign of their personality strength. However, such emotions are expressed in a mature and well-modulated fashion. So, at times of even intensely painful life events, high-functioning people may suffer a great deal, but they are still able to cope with major life issues (e.g., work, education, parenting, and relationships). As the old Timex commercial put it, these folks can "take a lickin' and keep on tickin'."

Resiliency

Resiliency is related to the ability to resist dysfunction. All of us have a limit to what we can endure and in the face of extremely severe or prolonged stressors, some impairment in functioning may occur. Even the strongest among us may become overwhelmed, at least for a while. However, another marker of ego strength is the ability to emotionally regroup and recover when major stressful events subside. This contrasts with those who function at lower levels of ego strength who may become seriously impaired (often in response even to mild-to-moderate stressors), and who remain quite symptomatic for a prolonged period of time after major stressors subside.

Finally, in emotionally resilient people, the clinician will be impressed by the continuing presence of many personal strengths despite their tremendous emotional suffering. One should never look solely at the amount of psychic pain as a barometer of ego functioning. We all have the capability of suffering a great deal when life is hard, or tragic, but those with solid egos keep on tickin'.

Decompensation

The concept of *decompensation* refers to the phenomenon of progressive breakdown or erosion of ego functioning when an individual is under stress. In people functioning at a high or neurotic level, decompensation does occur, but only in limited ways. Conversely, the hallmark of more severe psychopathology is a vulnerability to decompensation. Thus, those with more severe personality disorders are (a) more likely to show a deterioration in ego functioning, even in response to rather minor stressors, and (b) prone to a serious collapse of ego functioning (i.e., the degree of decompensation is more pronounced).

Case Examples:
Decompensation and the Issue of Ego Strength

Let's consider two people, Ms. N. and Ms. B. Ms. N. has adequately developed ego strength, and she functions at a neurotic level of adjustment. Ms. B.'s ego strength is marginal, and she functions at a borderline level. Scenario A illustrates ego functions for each under optimal circumstances (i.e., very low stress conditions and an intact social support system). The example is limited to only three ego functions: thought processes, reality testing, and control of emotions. (On this continuum, level 1 represents gross dysfunction while level 7 reflects mature, healthy ego functioning.)

Scenario A: Ego Functions Under Optimal Circumstances

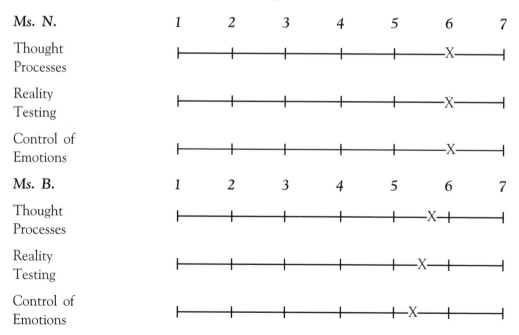

Under *optimal* conditions, neither is grossly symptomatic, although we must appreciate that Ms. B. is in a chronic state of vulnerability.

Scenario B shows a time when both women are subject to the same level of environmental stress; in this example, being laid off from work (certainly a very stressful, but generally not a catastrophic stressor). Let's see what happens to each in the wake of this stressor.

Scenario B: Ego Functions Under Moderate Stress

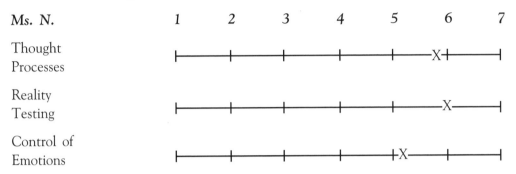

In Ms. N.'s case, there are essentially no changes in her ability to think logically and to perceive reality. We do see, however, some diminished ability to adaptively control her emotions. (With neurotics, either overcontainment of emotions or some degree of increased emotional lability is likely, but not pronounced dyscontrol.) Generally, in neurotic-level people, the only ego function that becomes noticeably impaired under mild-to-moderate stress is emotional control.

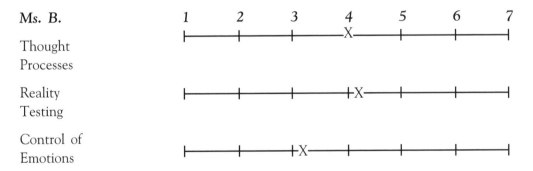

For Ms. B. the impact of stressors has resulted in a much more severe impairment in functioning. She now engages in a significant amount of black-or-white thinking and many conclusions are made in an arbitrary fashion. She often feels confused. She is more prone to misinterpreting certain aspects of reality (especially interpersonal interactions). Most notably, her emotional controls are seriously compromised and she experiences times of pronounced dyscontrol. Overall, the degree of erosion of ego functions is much more severe for Ms. B. than for Ms. N. Similarly, after the stressors have subsided for Ms. N., she will probably become asymptomatic again, while Ms. B. may continue to function at a lower level for a number of months—even if her job is reinstated. Neurotic-level people certainly feel the impact of stressful events, but they exhibit considerably better resistance and resiliency.

ASSESSMENT OF EGO STRENGTH: PRACTICAL ASPECTS

The "ego" is a hypothetical construct and as such is rather hard to define. The best way to approach this problem is to define the ego (and its strength) by noting specific ego functions that can be assessed by observing the client's behavior. Many authors have offered lists of ego functions; I shall present an abbreviated list that loosely parallels the model suggested by Bellack, et al. (1973). Bellack's group speaks of ego functions as existing on a continuum from mature, healthy, and adaptive (level 7) to immature, maladaptive, and grossly pathologic (level 1). Let's take a look at this schema by first focusing on the general continuum (see Figure 1.2), and then focusing specifically on four separate ego functions: thought processes, reality testing, defenses, and control of emotions and impulses. (See Table 1.1.)

THREE TYPES OF EMOTIONAL RESPONSES

A very useful model can help illustrate these particular ego functions. Developed by psychiatrist Mardi Horowitz and colleagues, this model is useful for understanding the experience of emotions and the resulting impact on personality functioning (Marmar 1991). According to Horowitz, people respond emotionally in one of three ways: *overcontrol, dyscontrol,* or *emotional tolerance.* See Figure 1.3.

Overcontrol

Overcontrol is a state of mind in which a person either automatically or consciously attempts to ward off the experience of a painful feeling. There may be cognitive acknowledgment of distressing events and some vague, inner awareness of unpleasant emotions. However, in a number of ways, the individual is backing away from experiencing the feelings head-on. Overcontrol is maintained by avoiding situations that potentially could trigger emotions, by using distractions (e.g., excessive involvement in work, keeping active, exercise, etc.), intellectualizing, rationalizing, denial, and minimizing (e.g., "It's no big deal," "Worse things have happened to others," "I can handle it"), or by emotional numbing (either by the abuse of substances or by defense mechanisms such as dissociation).

Overcontrol is a natural, normal way of responding to difficult and painful life events. It can serve adaptively by keeping emotions at bay. Yet, it can be carried to extremes and interfere with the processes of mourning and working through painful emotions.

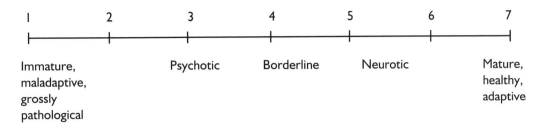

Figure 1.2. Continuum of Personality Functioning

Dyscontrol

Dyscontrol, conversely, is a state of mind in which the individual's defenses seriously fail. The person is overwhelmed by extremely intense emotions or impulses. It is important to emphasize that dyscontrol is much more than just *feeling* strong emotions. It represents a flooding of painful affects that are almost intolerable and potentially can result in severe fragmentation or disorganization of the personality. Most higher-functioning people never experience true dyscontrol, although particular life crises do evoke strong painful feelings. Dyscontrol is almost always seen in the context of ego weakness and severe psychopathology.

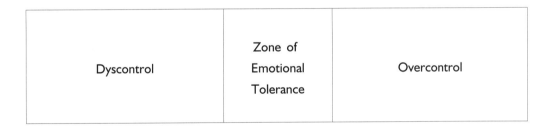

Figure 1.3. The Experience of Emotion

Emotional Tolerance

Emotional tolerance is a state of mind in which a person does, in fact, experience very strong emotions, and yet is able to tolerate the experience. In such instances, the individual may become flooded by sadness, fear, etc., which certainly may "feel" overwhelming, yet the experience does not lead to disorganization. The individual lives through waves of intense emotion, it passes, and then he or she re-enters a less intense state of mind.

Table 1.1.   Ego Functions

Level   Thought Processes

6–7:   Logical, realistic thinking. Good ability to problem solve, anticipate consequences.

4–6:   May exhibit concreteness or overgeneralized thinking (especially when under stress), e.g., all-or-none conclusions, arbitrary inferences, pessimistic predictions. However, thinking is logical and goal directed. Errors in thinking at this level include the often cited "cognitive distortions" proposed by Aaron Beck (1976) and other cognitive therapists.

2–4:   More extreme, arbitrary conclusions, lack of critical thinking; thinking tends to be impulsive without appropriate reflectiveness. Can present with magical thinking, ideas of reference, and quasi-delusional thinking.

1–2:   Severe fragmentation of thought processes, loose associations, confusion, profoundly unrealistic conclusions, delusions.

Level   Reality Testing (and Sense of Reality)

6–7:   Intact reality testing.

4–6:   Intact reality testing in most circumstances, however, some impairments seen in the context of intense relationships (e.g., transference reactions) or strong emotions (e.g., loss of perspective while in the midst of significant emotional arousal).

2–4:   Significant impairments in reality testing, e.g., grossly misreading social cues or interpersonal interactions, jumping to far-fetched conclusions. May experience transient illusions or hallucinations. Blurring of self–other boundaries. Derealization.

1–2:   Marked impairment in reality testing. Confusion, hallucinations.

Level   Defenses

6–7:   Defenses are employed only during times of intense stress. Defenses used are effective in warding off emotional dyscontrol and involve little or no distortion of reality. Defense operations typically include mild levels of denial, rationalization, intellectualization, humor, and distractions (e.g., playing sports, exercising, taking a weekend vacation). And, importantly, the degree of defensiveness is not extreme, so the individual can easily access, acknowledge, and express inner feelings when he/she chooses to do so.

4–6:   The hallmark of neurosis is an overreliance on defenses, i.e., various intrapsychic and interpersonal maneuvers designed to avoid experiencing or expressing inner emotional pain.

2–4: Defenses are brittle and often ineffective in warding off intense affective arousal. Defenses often involve significant impairment in reality testing (e.g., denial, projection, splitting, severe distortions). The dominant defenses are collectively referred to as "acting out"; i.e., desperate attempts to avoid awareness of inner emotional pain, such as severe substance abuse, self-mutilation, rampant promiscuity, binge eating, etc.

1–2: Marginal or no adequate defenses.

Level   **Control of Emotions and Impulses**

6–7: Exhibits both the ability to *appropriately* contain and control emotions *and* to choose to express feelings at the appropriate time and place (i.e., has the capacity to engage in healthy emotional expression, e.g., mourn losses, express frustration, etc.).

4–6: Two versions are seen at this level. The first is a degree of impaired emotional dyscontrol where the individual feels overwhelmed and may either express emotions in a maladaptive manner or experience a loss of control (e.g., break down crying at work). The second version is maladaptive overcontrol where the individual keeps a lid on emotional expression to an excessive degree. The result is difficulty in sharing feelings with others and a diminished capacity for appropriately working through painful emotional experiences. They are over-defended.

2–4: Again, two versions are seen: The first is severe emotional dysregulation. Individuals are exquisitely sensitive to stressors and respond to them with intense, poorly modulated outbursts of emotion (e.g., intense despair, rage, severe panic). The second version involves desperate attempts to contain intense affects, but it is a from of brittle control. The overcontrol often gives way to extreme emotional outbursts. In addition, the severe dyscontrol seen at this level may include suicidal, homicidal, and/or self-mutilation behaviors.

1–2: Marked emotional dyscontrol.

As you track moment-to-moment interactions during therapy sessions, you will be able to observe the dynamic ebb and flow between these different emotional states of mind.

Let's illustrate the model with three figures. Figure 1.4 shows Mr. A., a high-functioning, emotionally mature man who has recently lost his wife to breast cancer. He has the ego strength to contain most of his inner painful feelings during the day while he works as a general contractor. He is willing and able to speak openly about his emotional frame of mind with his two grown children, however; and he can cry with them when, in privacy, they talk about their loss. At such times, he often experiences

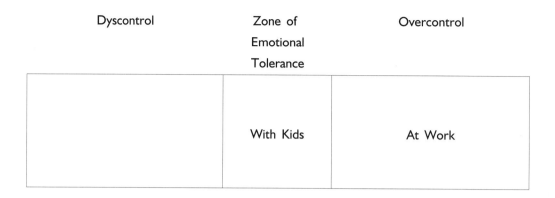

Figure 1.4. Mr. A's Emotional Experience

intense sadness, but he feels secure enough to share this sadness with his kids, and almost never feels completely out of control. Often, after talking with his children and weeping, he feels better. His experience is that his strong feelings make sense; he loved his wife, he misses her terribly, and the shared sadness leaves him feeling close to his children. Does he need therapy? Probably not.

In contrast, Mr. B. who has also lost his wife, has never felt comfortable with strong feelings. He grew up experiencing a significant amount of shame regarding the expression of emotions and has developed a characterological stance that can be described as rigid and overcontrolled. On the rare occasions when he has "broken down" he felt intense sadness, but never true dyscontrol. In the aftermath of these emotional moments, he felt anxious and a degree of humiliation. He has the capacity to feel his emotions and enough ego strength to tolerate them. But he doesn't trust them and is committed to keeping a lid on his feelings. He doesn't want to "burden" his kids with his strong feelings and prefers to be "strong for them." (See Figure 1.5.)

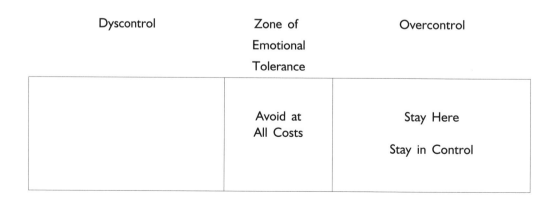

Figure 1.5. Mr. B's Emotional Experience

Should Mr. B. enter psychotherapy, a major goal would be to help him loosen the grip on his extreme defenses and support him in making contact with his inner, truer emotional self. Because he's neurotic, he may be afraid of intense feelings, but ultimately he would find that he could endure them, and real emotional healing could then begin as he more openly mourned his loss.

Finally, Figure 1.6 shows Mr. C.'s emotional experience. Mr. C. has also lost his wife. He is a man who has always functioned at a borderline level. His capacity for experiencing strong feelings in an adaptive way is almost nil.

In Figure 1.6 we see that Mr. C. has absolutely no zone of emotional tolerance. Thus, he grits his teeth and tries to avoid many sources of stress, especially situations or thoughts that might remind him of his loss and his current state of loneliness. Often, these attempts are unsuccessful and he plunges into a state of extreme despair. He describes such times as "being engulfed in overwhelming blackness and panic." These times are overwhelming and always provoke strong reactions (e.g., on a number of occasions he has flown into rages, breaking furniture and threatening his children).

Dyscontrol	Overcontrol
Either Here	Or Here

Figure 1.6. Mr. C's Emotional Experience

Once, he recounted feeling a sudden, intense sense of panic. "I thought I was going to lose my mind ... I felt shaky and a strange urge to smash my fist through a window. I did dig my fingernails into my arm until I started to bleed ... I went to my bedroom, drank a two-liter bottle of wine, and passed out." It is not surprising that he is often plagued with recurring thoughts about suicide.

A psychotherapeutic approach geared to help Mr. C. "get in touch with his feelings" is very likely to push him into dyscontrol, with disastrous consequences. We must first help this man to become more stabilized. The treatment must help him to shore up his faltering defenses and, in general, to improve ego functioning before any attempts are made to explore his intense feelings of sorrow and loss.

This particular model of the experience of emotion can be especially useful for therapists to track moment-to-moment experiences in therapy sessions. There is a continuous dynamic ebb and flow as clients talk and shift back and forth between these three main states of affective experiencing. More will be said about the use of this model in later sections of this chapter.

Many authors include additional ego functions to their assessments of ego strength. Two in particular will be addressed in detail: the development of self and level of interpersonal relatedness. At this point, however, let's sum up. As people encounter difficult times, they must tap into inner adaptive resources (i.e., ego functions) and will have greater or lesser degrees of success in coming to terms with their current life circumstances. The ego functions of thought processes, reality testing, defenses, and control of emotions and impulses can serve as markers or barometers for the therapist to assess on an ongoing basis. Aside from reports of subjective distress and particular symptoms, keeping a close watch on the ebbs and flows of ego functions can be a good way to monitor a patient's current state and to track improvement.

ASSESSING EGO FUNCTIONS

There are four main sources of data for assessing ego functions. They are as follows:

1. History: interpersonal, academic, and occupational functioning

2. "Red Flag" symptoms

3. Within-session markers

4. Between-session markers

Patients' Histories

The patient's history is the first area to assess for ego functioning. Since true BPD clients have an ingrained, persistent type of psychopathology, the history often can provide important data. It is very difficult to maintain stable functioning if one is plagued by severe, ongoing ego impairment. Thus, almost all borderline patients have what some have called a "checkered history." This appears especially in two areas:

- *Interpersonal relationships* (the rule is that for BPDs, personal relationships have been very unstable, marked by numerous intense involvements, rejections, and generally the absence of a sustained, committed relationship).

- *Academic and/or occupational functioning* (the chaotic performance, impulsivity, poor reality testing, etc. make it very difficult for BPD people to sustain productive employment or to achieve academically. Their histories often reveal multiple job changes, firings, and so forth).

It should be noted that *some* higher-level BPD patients have been able to achieve in school or find a niche occupationally where the structure of daily routines provides an island of stability. Thus, when taking a history, a report of chaotic, tumultuous interpersonal relationships generally carries more diagnostic weight.

A history of several years of good functioning (e.g., a stable relationship or occupational success) may contraindicate BPD. Most borderline people cannot maintain adequate functioning this long. Thus, if you see what appears to be borderline symptoms yet the individual has a history of good functioning, it is important to consider that the primary pathology may be caused by an Axis I disorder (e.g., substance abuse, bipolar disorder, etc.).

"Red Flag" Symptoms

The symptom history may reveal certain "red flags" that increase the index of suspicion that you are dealing with a borderline client. These symptoms/problems include (but are not limited to) the following:

■ Suicide attempts

■ Self-mutilation

■ Psychotic symptoms

■ Antisocial behavior, especially violence

■ Severe substance abuse

■ Marked sexual promiscuity or perverse sexual behaviors

Note that some of these symptoms are seen in the context of Axis I disorders, and do not always reflect borderline pathology.

Within- and Between-Session Markers

The final sources of data for assessing ego functioning are within-session and between-session markers. The symptom history certainly can alert us to borderline pathology, but a more important source of data is behavior that is noted from moment to moment. At times, this is revealed when the patient begins to experience significant emotional pain, and we observe signs of emotional dyscontrol (e.g., intense anger, panic, overwhelming despair). This dyscontrol may be accompanied by a breakdown in reality testing and thought processes (e.g., the client jumps to very unrealistic conclusions about what is happening in the session). Behavioral dyscontrol may occur; for example, the client may become verbally abusive or physically assaultive towards the therapist, he/she may bolt from the room, or engage in self-mutilation during the session. For example, one borderline client I treated began to bite himself severely during a session. Often strong reactions emerge that are directed toward the therapist; for example, the client will lash out at the therapist and make devaluing or abusive statements.

Extreme emotional within-session behaviors certainly occur, but more often what is seen is that, when overwhelmed during therapy, BPD clients leave the session and decompensate. Later, the therapist hears about overwhelming emotional despair or rampant acting out (e.g., severe alcohol abuse or self-mutilation). In extreme instances, there may be suicide attempts or the client may decide to completely drop out of treatment. All of these within- and between-session markers are reflections of marginal ego functioning.

All in all, when emotional experiences within sessions become too intense, the client loses the capacity to process the feelings, and under these circumstances the therapy itself may be experienced as traumatic.

Thus, the diagnosis of BPD is not based solely on presenting symptoms. The clinician must assess the current level of ego functioning and be alert to symptomatic "red flags." Beyond this, the history is quite important, as are the careful observations made during the course of therapy. Many borderline individuals are recognized within the first few minutes of the initial session. However, with many of these clients the full picture of their underlying psychopathology does not become apparent until the therapist has treated them for a while, and more subtle manifestations of the disorder emerge.

Let's now move on to explore several other important dimensions relevant to the diagnostic process.

DIAGNOSTIC ISSUES: DISORDERS OF THE "SELF"

An important area of psychological functioning is what people experience as an internal sense of "self." This is a somewhat illusive and hard-to-define construct, but it is a tremendously important aspect of one's psychological life. Almost always, individuals functioning at a borderline level exhibit aspects of an underdeveloped self.

It is rare that clients come into therapy exclaiming that "my SELF is underdeveloped." However, if we listen carefully to our clients, numerous outward signs of an impaired self can be identified. This will become more concrete if you examine the eleven areas listed in Table 1.2, in which we may get glimpses of the client's self.

It is important to note here that many people show signs of an underdeveloped self (i.e., it is not exclusively a problem with borderline disorders), although it is certainly a common element of borderline pathology.

The therapist's ability to spot signs of strength or the emergence of higher levels of ego development is tremendously important in treating BPD clients. Noticing these signs can be a good way to mark progress and pointing them out to clients is a powerful way to support their growth. During sessions, many comments are made that touch on the eleven areas listed in Table 1.2. Let's consider a few examples that may stand out as signs of the emerging self.

- A female client says, "He and I absolutely did not agree on how to handle this situation." (This statement reveals (1) an awareness of her own beliefs and point of view and (2) a defined boundary between herself and the other person.)

- Client: "I just had this gut feeling that he didn't really give a damn about me." Therapist: "So you trusted your intuition."

- Client: "I feel like I had a right to be upset about it—she was being very degrading." Therapist: "You felt that your reaction was legitimate?" Client: "Yes!"

- Client: "No matter what she said, I felt like I did a lot to help out and I feel proud of myself."

These are good signs to see during sessions, since they often signal a strengthening or growth of the self. It is easy to notice the chaos, the pain, the out-of-control behavior, and to miss the signs of emerging strength. Successful treatment for clients with BPD requires therapists to develop their skills in noticing and acknowledging ego strengths.

Table 1.2. Development of the SELF

Well-Developed SELF	Underdeveloped SELF
1. Awareness of inner beliefs, needs, values, feelings.	1. Unaware of inner needs, etc. or only vaguely perceived.
2. Feels a sense of "ownership" of inner needs, feelings, etc. Often experienced as understandable and legitimate (even when unpleasant).	2. Feelings or needs are often experienced as "happening *to* me" (not from within myself); may be perceived as ego-alien; may be disowned.
3. Can retain values, beliefs, feelings, and needs even when in the presence of powerful others.	3. Likely to abandon inner beliefs, needs, etc., quickly compromising to placate others. (This may or may not be experienced consciously or as a choice.)
4. Can make clear, unambiguous statements of inner feelings beliefs, needs, etc.	4. Expressions of inner feelings are often cloaked in hesitancy, apologies, or minimization.
5. A constant inner sense of "I" or "SELF" across a broad array of situations/circumstances.	5. An ill-defined sense of inner self or constantly shifting, fragmented sense of self. The person often is confused about how he or she really feels or what he or she really wants.
6. Pursues personally meaningful goals; life is lived in accord with inner desires and values.	6. Occupational and other major life pursuits are ill-defined, chaotic, or undirected. There is a lack of clarity regarding major life goals and decisions.
7. An inner sense of "centered-ness" analogous to an anchor or ballast in a ship that provides an experience of stability, especially during stressful times.	7. An internal sense of chaos, fragmentation, and instability.
8. Clear self-other boundaries. Able to be empathic yet also maintain separateness.	8. Very permeable boundaries. An example is when another person is sad, BPD clients so resonate with the other, that they too become sad.
9. Able to internally self-generate feelings of worth.	9. Inordinate reliance on others to provide reassurance.
10. Can take an assertive stand on things that matter.	10. Passivity or subjugation. Quickly abandons own beliefs, needs, etc.
11. Trusts hunches and intuitive feelings.	11. Unaware of or discounts hunches and intuitions.

DIAGNOSTIC ISSUES: IMMATURE LEVELS OF RELATEDNESS

If you only had one word to describe severe personality disorders, it would probably be *immaturity*. This is certainly seen in the realm of affective control. It is also a major defining aspect of patterns of interpersonal relating. Again consider a continuum. On the healthy end are the individuals who can form intimate connections. Capable of empathy, altruism, and commitment, they are able to establish relationships based on trust, give and take, and they genuinely care about the welfare of the other, independent of their own personal needs.

At the extreme pathological end are people who are either profoundly detached (e.g., severe schizoids) or those who enter relationships only to use or hurt the other (e.g., antisocial personalities; malignant narcissists).

Neurotic clients often come to therapy complaining of problems in relationships that include the following: difficulties with intimacy (e.g., feeling inhibited about intimacy, or conversely, having chronic feelings of loneliness and longing for more in important relationships), ambivalence regarding commitment, feelings of jealousy or competitiveness, feeling inadequate in the presence of overpowering people, or experiencing difficulties in clearly communicating with others. However, despite these problems, most neurotic people basically do have the desire and the capacity to love others.

For most borderline-level clients, however, interpersonal relations are a source of tremendously intense pleasure and pain. Marked egocentricity is a defining characteristic of borderline personality disorder. Despite what some BPD people call "true love" for others, most often the reality is that their relationships are based on "need gratification" (i.e., the central feature is wanting, needing, and demanding that "I come first" and that the other exists only to meet their needs). This intensely egocentric level of relating can be seen in numerous behaviors exhibited by borderline clients, including the following:

- *Very* strong reactions to separation or rejection

- Tremendous difficulties being alone

- Manipulative suicidal gestures in response to interpersonal stresses

- Fits of temper or rage when others do not meet their needs

- A tendency to fall in love quickly or to idealize others; yet rapid shifts into anger or devaluation if others do not meet their needs

- Profound obliviousness to the needs of others

- Clinginess, helplessness, neediness

■ Difficulties ending therapy sessions on time and the tendency to make multiple calls to therapists between sessions

What continues to amaze me is how many people are able to achieve and function on a high level cognitively (and even professionally) yet show clear evidence of borderline pathology, especially noticeable in the areas of affect control and immature levels of relating. Don't be caught off guard. Having a Ph.D., C.P.A., C.E.O., or an M.D. after a name, or any other outward signs of "success" does not always mean that the person is fully mature.

> **Case Example:** Dr. X. was a highly successful and respected consultant to engineering corporations. He authored many books, not only on engineering, but also on corporate management and organizational dynamics. His IQ clearly was 140 plus and he had a way of impressing people at first glance. Most who know him informally would describe him as a high-energy, brilliant dynamo. In the arena of work and especially when he was showered with praise and in control, he excelled. However, on a more private level he often experienced times of considerable emotional turmoil. In particular, if he was ever outdone by a fellow consultant or on the rare occasion when his advice proved to be incorrect, he would fall into a state of extreme desperation. He would become flooded with thoughts of suicide. Often he coped with such times by heavy drinking and by what he called his "escapist fantasies." After many months of therapy he reluctantly told the therapist that his fantasies included highly sadistic scenarios where he would tie up his enemies (e.g., competitors) and torture them. The details are too gruesome to recount. He also confessed, ashamedly, that during these fantasies he became sexually aroused.
>
> Most people saw Dr. X. as temperamental and egotistical, but no one knew of his secret life of despair and fantasized revenge.

Evidence of the client's level of interpersonal relatedness can certainly be gleaned from the client's description of problems in past and current relationships. An even more direct way to assess this level is to observe what unfolds in the context of the therapeutic relationship.

DIAGNOSTIC ISSUES: PRIMITIVE THEMES

In lower-functioning BPD patients, the psychopathology is hard to ignore. Yet in higher-level borderline disorders, it may not be immediately apparent. As mentioned earlier, many of these clients have been seen as "neurotic," until the emergence of more clear-cut signs of serious pathology. What can bleed through seeming normalcy is what I call "primitive themes"—symptoms, behaviors, comments, and other observable signs that alert the clinician "you have just entered borderline territory." In many respects, these behaviors are associated with ego impairment, poorly developed sense of self, and the immature modes of interpersonal relatedness discussed in earlier sections. For some clients, such themes dominate their lives; for others, they erupt only occasionally, at times of significant stress. Seven common indicators of primitive themes are listed below:

- Magical thinking, e.g., assuming that the therapist somehow intuitively knows how they feel or what they need, even though that feeling or need has not been verbalized by the client.

- The expectation that the therapist is continuously available to meet their needs (e.g., expecting the therapist to be readily available in the middle of the night and being offended if the therapist is not eager to speak with them at 3 a.m.).

- Entitlement—that is, a sense of astonishment or outrage when the client's needs are not fully met. Also feeling entitled to special treatment (e.g., free psychotherapy, unlimited phone calls, extended length of sessions, etc.).

- Extremely intense transference reactions without awareness of the inappropriateness of the reaction, e.g., a client lashes out at the therapist and accuses her of being a "cold bitch" despite the fact that the therapist has always been very warm and supportive. Note: Neurotic patients certainly can exhibit intense transference reactions, although they have good enough reality testing to appreciate that their reactions may be overly intense or inappropriate given the reality of the client-therapist relationship. Borderline people frequently reveal intense transference reactions and yet fail to see them as inappropriate.

- Markedly unrealistic expectations or demands that the therapist quickly take away their pain or somehow rapidly solve serious, long-standing problems.

- A loss of empathy revealed by the client's seeming obliviousness to the needs and feelings of others (including the therapist).

- Bizarre behaviors, fantasies, or ideations. For example, a priest I once treated mentioned in an off-the-cuff manner that the only way he could become sexually aroused was to insert pliers in his rectum. Another example is of a woman client who often thought about taking a needle and dissecting the tendons in her wrist. A student intern once reported to me that her client, at the end of a session, turned to her, thanked her, and abruptly licked her on the forehead. Neurotics don't behave in such a bizarre fashion.

DIAGNOSTIC ISSUES: OTHER CHARACTERISTICS RELATED TO DIAGNOSIS, PROGNOSIS, AND TREATMENT PLANS

Beyond a formal diagnosis and an assessment of the level of functioning, a number of other variables are very important to consider. The following ten factors often influence treatment outcome significantly.

1. The presence or absence of significant substance abuse. This is probably the single most critical variable. Those BPD clients who continue to abuse alcohol or other substances, as a group, have been shown to have a much poorer prognosis.

2. Degree of psychological mindedness. This is the capacity and willingness to look within (i.e., to become aware of and share inner thoughts, feelings, impulses, etc.). Some people are simply unable to do this. Psychological mindedness may be a characteristic that is independent of diagnosis, e.g., some borderline patients may be much more able to engage in this type of introspection than some rigid, overly defended neurotics.

3. Level of intellectual functioning. People who are of below average intelligence or those who are simply concrete thinkers may not respond well to many therapeutic interventions.

4. The courage to face emotional pain. Despite extreme emotional sensitivity and inadequate defenses, some borderline individuals exhibit tremendous courage to face unpleasant realities and painful inner feelings. I have often felt a good deal of admiration for those clients who, despite their limitations, find the ability to face significantly painful material.

5. Sense of humor.

6. Degree of development of a superego (conscience).

7. Likability and friendliness.

8. The ability to own up to their role in creating problems (versus the tendency to externalize blame and dodge personal responsibility).

9. The presence or absence of a concurrent Axis I disorder (e.g., panic disorder, depression, bipolar disorder, etc.).

10. The presence or absence of a social support network (friends, relatives, church, community, etc.).

All therapists encounter people who are clearly borderline, yet who respond well to treatment. Often this is the result of some positive personality characteristics such as those outlined above.

DIAGNOSTIC ISSUES: SUMMARY CONCLUSIONS AND DIFFERENTIAL DIAGNOSIS

After the first session, it is helpful to review the various diagnostic issues outlined in this chapter. To aid in this process, I have provided, on page 34, a diagnostic summary checklist. This is also a useful tool to track progress during treatment and may be a helpful guide when submitting reports to insurance companies.

Differential Diagnosis

I would like to briefly highlight the markers that distinguish borderline disorders, from other levels of psychopathology; I will consider the continuum from the high-level, mature individual to a very severe level of psychopathology. (See Figure 1.7.)

1. **Mature, high-functioning people:** Have a solidly developed sense of self, good ego functioning, and the capacity to develop mature, intimate relationships. When these people encounter major life stresses they certainly suffer feelings of loss, sadness, frustration, anxiety, etc. However, they are emotionally sturdy, rarely decompensate, and are able to engage in various processes that facilitate emotional healing, e.g., they can be open to their pain, can share feelings with trusted others, can maintain social supports, and can take productive action to resolve life problems.

2. **Neurotic-level personalities:** For most neurotics, basic ego functions are relatively well developed. However, they tend to cope with life crises by an overuse of defenses. When under stress, most neurotics, in a sense, grit their teeth and overcontrol inner emotions. This results in difficulties in facing painful inner truths and can prolong the process of emotionally working through difficult experiences. These people often encounter problems in interpersonal relationships (e.g., competitiveness, inhibited assertiveness, intimacy difficulties), but fundamentally, they are capable of and desirous of establishing loving relationships. Many have developed a "self," although often what is experienced is what many authors call a "false self" (i.e., a self molded to fit the demands and expectations of others). Thus, many neurotics come to see this persona as their "self" and may be only vaguely aware of an underlying more authentic self. Severe decompensation in this group is rare.

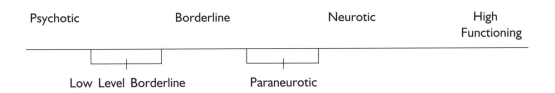

Figure 1.7. Continuum of Personality Functioning

3. **Borderline-level personalities:** Although the specific clinical presentation can vary a lot, all borderline-level people share the following common characteristics: significant ego weakness (especially in the area of emotional and impulse control, manifest by extreme affective sensitivity, reactivity, and impulsivity), an immature level of interpersonal relatedness (best characterized as egocentric), and a poorly developed sense of self. Borderline people are very emotionally vulnerable and prone to significant decompensation in the face of even minor stressors.

   Note: Lower-functioning borderlines are more prone to self-mutilation, dangerous acting out, and transient psychotic symptoms.

4. **Psychotic-level personalities:** Such individuals (many of whom are schizophrenic) are very prone to severe decompensation. Psychotic reactions in this group typically are not transient. When present, psychosis may continue for months. Almost always, these people have a very poorly developed sense of self and are incapable of establishing meaningful relationships outside of their immediate family.

Table 1.3. Continuum of Personality Functioning

	Ego Functions	Defense Mechanisms	Dominated by "Old Pain" (1)	Experience of "Self"
High-Functioning Individuals	Adequate	Appropriate	No	Adequate
Neurotic Level	Adequate	Defense too rigid	Yes	(2)
Borderline Level	Impaired	Inadequate	Yes	Inadequate
Psychotic Level	Grossly impaired	Grossly inadequate	Yes	Grossly inadequate

1. High-functioning individuals are not burdened by major unhealed wounds from the past. They have adequately worked through such issues. Their sources of emotional pain are due mainly to stressful events occurring in present-day life. Conversely, lower-level people are much more prone to experience suffering not only from here-and-now events, but also to pain emanating from traumatic events in their past. This is manifested either in painful memories of past interactions and/or increased vulnerability such that current events that resemble past painful circumstances simply hurt more.

2. Neurotic-level people have a self, but may be dominated by a "false self", i.e., a self that has been largely fashioned out of compliance to others (i.e., not a "real self").

Paraneurotics

It is important to note yet another group of people. These individuals straddle the line between neurosis and borderline and represent a fairly large group of people treated in mental health settings. This group has been described in the literature, but no one has invented a term to designate it (maybe we could call them paraneurotics, pseudo-neurotics, wanna be neurotics, or borderline lite). Regardless of nomenclature, this is a real group of patients that needs to be recognized. They may, in the midst of a *significant* life crisis or an Axis I disorder, reveal what looks like borderline traits or symptoms. However, two features distinguish them from true borderline people.

■   The first is that they do not present the more typical chaotic, unstable history seen in most borderline people. They have been able to establish relationships and function relatively well for prolonged periods of time. The decompensation and emergence of borderline symptoms has occurred only recently in the wake of significant stressors or life crises.

> Mahler and Kaplan (1977) introduced the term "sub-phase inadequacy" to describe clients who were not clearly borderline but were prone to fairly significant regression when under stress. The term derives from object relations theory that holds that solid ego development depends on adequate experiences during pre-oedipal sub-phases of development. Significant developmental problems during these early stages of life can result in borderline pathology. Somewhat less severe difficulties may not totally derail development, and ego formation proceeds, but it leaves the individual with "sub-phase deficiencies" that remain in the form of psychological vulnerabilities. Blanck and Blanck (1979, p. 67) state "that sub-phase problems can persist in neurotic structure has been sensed for a long time without conceptualization. Mahler gave it substance in her description of [sub-phase inadequacy]." They consider two forms of neurosis, structural neurosis and neurosis that is "sub-phase burdened."

■   The second distinguishing feature is that when the stress subsides or there is a resolution of an Axis I disorder (e.g., a major depressive episode), if you go looking for borderline features, you won't find them.

These patients in all likelihood are not true borderline clients, but rather people who have experienced significant regression in response either to severe stress (e.g., post-traumatic stress disorder) or to neurochemically mediated, Axis I disorders. Data varies, but approximately 50 to 75 percent of patients initially diagnosed with a major Axis I disorder and BPD do not look borderline when seen several years after the initial episode (Stone, Hurt, et al. 1988).

This should give us pause before labeling someone as "borderline." The best way to make the distinction between this group and true borderline patients rests on two sources of data: (1) the history and (2) the presence of a number of very positive personality attributes, even in the midst of some more pathological symptoms.

These distinctions are not just academic. Rather, they are important diagnostic distinctions that will guide the therapist in making treatment decisions (initial, general treatment strategies and goals, and interventions that address the constantly shifting clinical picture seen from session to session).

SYMPTOMATIC EBBS AND FLOWS

Borderline people do show a chronic history of affective and interpersonal instability. However, it is important to appreciate that there is a significant degree of fluctuation seen over time with regard to symptomology and functional impairments. This concept has been highlighted by Gunderson (1975), who emphasizes how *contextual variables* can play a crucial role in influencing the severity of symptoms at any given point in time. He describes three general sets of interpersonal circumstances that play a role in determining the patient's level of functioning. Let us first assume that borderline clients are in a state of continuous vulnerability and are prone to dramatic shifts in ability to function if situational/interpersonal factors change.

1. Generally, the highest level of functioning is seen when the person is in a fairly supportive relationship. More florid symptoms are absent under these conditions. However, inner subjective experiences reveal that not all is O.K. Despite the relative stability in their current interpersonal world, the borderline person is often plagued by feelings of boredom, emptiness, loneliness, and despair. Self-esteem is tenuous and there is the ever-present worry about "the other leaving me." The preoccupation with anticipated or fantasized abandonment leads not only to ongoing anxiety and depressive feelings, but also to a common tendency to subjugate the self. This may be seen as an interpersonal maneuver designed to ensure permanence in a key relationship. It often takes the form of an excessive amount of compromise, being or becoming whatever the other person wants or needs, and ignoring their own needs, feelings, and beliefs. This style of subjugation can be an ongoing experience that thwarts the growth of the real self in a major way. Sometimes, it is also manifested in clinginess and difficulties in being alone. On the surface, many borderline individuals under these conditions appear to function normally (at least from an outsider's perspective).

> **Bipolar Disorder and Borderline Personality Disorder**
>
> Affective instability is the hallmark of both bipolar disorder and borderline personality disorder (BPD). It is important to make the differential diagnosis. Sometimes this diagnostic distinction is difficult, especially if the client has bipolar II disorder or dysphoric mania. The mood lability seen with bipolar disorder is often provoked by psychosocial stressors. However, in a careful review of the course of illness, there is a much greater chance of some spontaneous episodes (i.e., emerging in the absence of stressors) in bipolar versus BPD. Additionally, in most BPD patients, there is a long history of extreme responses to real or imagined abandonment or to interpersonal separations. Bipolar and BPD can also be co-morbid diagnoses. A recent international consensus panel addressing this issue recommended that if a patient meets criteria for both disorders the clinician should treat the bipolar illness with mood stabilizers (e.g., lithium or divalproex) (Gunderson 2003).

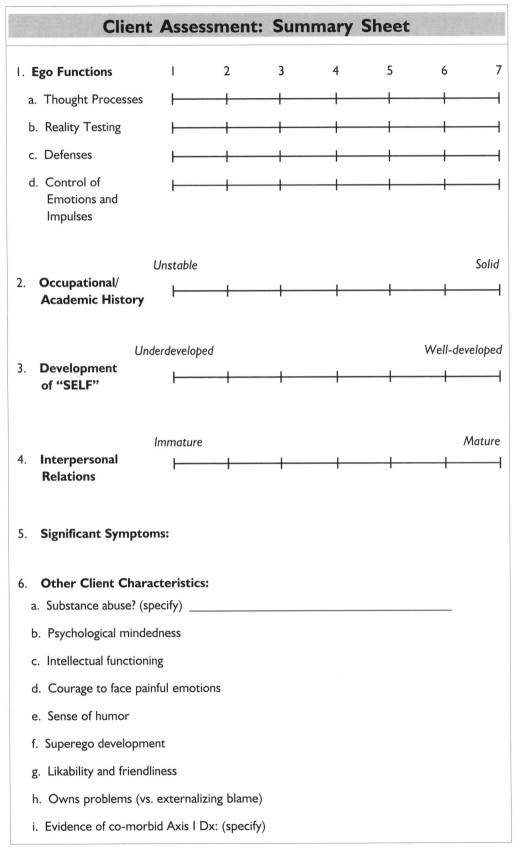

Client Assessment: Summary Sheet

1. **Ego Functions**   1   2   3   4   5   6   7

   a. Thought Processes

   b. Reality Testing

   c. Defenses

   d. Control of
      Emotions and
      Impulses

                 Unstable   *Solid*

2. **Occupational/
   Academic History**

        Underdeveloped   *Well-developed*

3. **Development
   of "SELF"**

         Immature   *Mature*

4. **Interpersonal
   Relations**

5. **Significant Symptoms:**

6. **Other Client Characteristics:**

   a. Substance abuse? (specify) _____

   b. Psychological mindedness

   c. Intellectual functioning

   d. Courage to face painful emotions

   e. Sense of humor

   f. Superego development

   g. Likability and friendliness

   h. Owns problems (vs. externalizing blame)

   i. Evidence of co-morbid Axis I Dx: (specify)

2. When the primary relationship is unstable or deteriorating, another set of circumstances occurs that plays a crucial role in the severity of symptoms. In such cases, the threat of separation, loss, and abandonment has become more likely. This can have a profoundly destabilizing effect on borderline people. Here is where we see the emergence of more intense symptoms and regression. At this level, there may be either the breakthrough of intense anger, irritability, devaluation, and rage or (probably more often) desperate feelings of depression and panic. Often there is a vacillation between outer-directed anger and then collapse into self-loathing and despair. Emotional controls erode, and feelings are expressed in volatile and very maladaptive ways. (Such volatility often serves only to push others away and create distance, which then heightens fears of abandonment; obviously a vicious cycle is set in motion.)

   Desperate attempts to maintain contact with a significant other may include pronounced clinging and manipulative suicidal gestures (the intent being to coerce the other to re-establish contact out of guilt feelings). Substance abuse is often seen as an attempt to quell intensely painful emotions.

3. The most distressing contextual variable occurs when there is actual loss of the other or abandonment. This can precipitate severe decompensation. The result is intense affect storms (rage, panic, feelings of emptiness, depression) and defenses against the pain (e.g., severe and dangerous acting out). Lower-level borderlines may exhibit self-mutilation, suicide attempts (with more lethal intent), and transient psychotic symptoms.

What is clear from these descriptions is that many borderline people (although not all) are profoundly dependent, and, generally, interpersonal rejections and losses are the most toxic set of stressors that they can encounter. Rejection or loss is the Achilles heel of most borderline patients.

Unfortunately, the general chaos and intensity seen in borderline patients is extremely maladaptive in that it often is a major factor in provoking repeated experiences of rejection, loss, and abandonment. Not too many friends, relatives, or employers can endure the intense emotions that frequently erupt. To further complicate issues, as the borderline patient becomes severely impaired, occupational functioning may deteriorate, thus eroding one additional source of stability.

Psychologist Jeffrey Young has proposed a different model that helps to explain the shifts in behavior often seen in borderline clients. He suggests that many borderline patients, in ways somewhat similar to that seen in multiple personality disorder, experience various "personalities" in response to certain precipitating events. You can see shifts from one personality to another from session to session, or within a single session. He calls these modes. They are not distinct personalities such as those that are more characteristic of MPD, but rather are states of mind that involve the following: certain affective states, styles of interpersonal relating, certain predominate cognitions, self-schemas, and areas of emotional vulnerability. Young describes seven commonly encountered modes (1996):

1. **The Vulnerable Child:** In this mode, the client often appears to be quite helpless, scared, and emotionally overwhelmed. A sub-type of the vulnerable child is the "abandoned child."

2. **The Angry Child:** This mode is evident as the client shifts to a defensive, irritable, and angry posture. Clients often express strong feelings of anger directed towards others who have been perceived as uncaring or hurtful (including the therapist). Anger is generally intense and expressed in maladaptive ways.

3. **The Detached Protector:** This mode is devoted to cutting off feelings and needs. Either the client literally feels nothing or makes statements such as "I don't need you—I don't need anyone!" Other versions of this mode include the overuse of alcohol or other drugs in an attempt to create a numbing effect, states of dissociation, a submissive-compliant interpersonal stance, and/or excessive overcontrol. (This is often accompanied by the emergence of psychosomatic symptoms.)

4. **The Punitive, Critical Parent:** This may be understood as introjects of harsh parents. It is manifested behaviorally in the form of self-hatred, self-blame, self-disgust. Young speculates that this is related to early experiences with parents who punished the child for expressing feelings or needs.

5. **Overcompensator:** In this mode, the person will show evidence of excessive and unrealistic standards for himself/herself. This mode is especially common in clients with narcissistic features. High expectations (possibly to defend against and overcome inner feelings of profound worthlessness) motivate frantic efforts to succeed, and failure to meet goals can evoke intense shame and humiliation.

6. **The Spontaneous Child:** This is a nonpathological mode in which a person is able to more freely experience and express basic human needs and emotions.

7. **The Healthy Adult:** This is the mode that therapy attempts to foster, in which the person can interact with others in the world in a more mature and adaptive fashion.

Case Example: Let's consider one common situation. During a therapy session, Lucy begins to gradually reveal intensely painful feelings of loneliness and neediness. She is tearful and has the demeanor of a hurt child. (She is in the vulnerable child mode.) Then, there is a rather sudden shift, as she remarks, "God, what's wrong with me? You must be sick of hearing this shit. I'm just *so* disgusted with myself" (punitive, critical parent mode). Obviously, she is the same person, but her experience of herself changes significantly as she flips into another mode.

Young strongly suggests that although therapists must provide consistency in many respects (e.g., maintaining the therapeutic frame), it is also critical to provide different kinds of interventions depending on which mode is present in the moment. For example, in the angry child mode, especially if there is a loss of control and the patient is becoming explosive or violent, firmness and limit setting may be necessary. However, an overly firm stance and strict limit setting may not be appropriate when the client is in the vulnerable child mode. Such firmness may be experienced as punitive or rejecting. In this mode, it may be much more necessary to be gentle and empathic. Gabbard (in the Menninger Treatments Outcome Study; 1996a) has echoed this view, stating that successful therapists were found to be those who maintained general consistency and limits, but also were highly flexible in their interventions. Nonsuccessful therapists tended to be too rigid and inflexible.

Symptoms come and go. It is the history of recurrent instability that really counts and makes the diagnosis more precise.

CO-MORBIDITY AND THE RELEVANCE OF DIAGNOSTICS

In many respects there is a two-way street between Axis I and Axis II disorders. As noted previously, a number of people may exhibit borderline features as they regress in the face of serious Axis I disorders. Conversely, the tremendous, ongoing vulnerability experienced by borderline clients makes them high risk for repeated Axis I disorders (especially major depression and substance abuse). Data varies across studies, but anywhere from 25 to 75 percent of borderline patients also have a co-morbid Axis I disorder. As will be addressed in the chapters on treatment, it is very important to treat Axis I disorders in BPD aggressively—especially if we are to have any chance of helping borderline people with shorter-term therapy.

For decades, some mental health professionals have strongly opposed the process of "diagnosing patients," seeing this exercise as dehumanizing. There are persuasive arguments that diagnostic pigeonholing can interfere with our ability to truly understand our clients. I think these beliefs have some merit, *and* I also see an important role for diagnosis. If all psychotherapy clients could be treated successfully with the same set of techniques, diagnosing might become a moot exercise. However, this is absolutely not the case. Many of these severely wounded, fragile people can be (and are) harmed by therapeutic approaches that would be perfectly appropriate for use with higher-functioning clients. For example, much of the psychotherapy literature focuses on techniques designed to increase awareness of inner feelings, to open people up, and to promote insight. Often these approaches are the centerpiece of treatment for neurotics, but they can seriously destabilize borderline patients.

If at all possible, it is desirable to formulate a working diagnostic hypothesis during the first session, especially when doing brief therapy, particularly because this will relate to setting limits, establishing a contract, and avoiding catastrophes. Ideally, therapists need at least some idea of the client's level of functioning by the end of the first session. There is no reason that this must interfere with providing an accepting and empathic relationship with the client. In fact, clear understanding of what is happening allows us to approach therapy in an informed way and ultimately enables us to provide more effective treatment.

Although generally the diagnosis is made based on careful history taking and clinical interview, psychological tests may at times be useful. Where this has special relevance is in the superficially competent person, but one whom you suspect may harbor an underlying borderline disorder (see appendix A).

PART II

ETIOLOGY

CHAPTER 2

Etiological Issues

GENERAL CONSIDERATIONS

Theories of etiology attempt to make sense of complex phenomena. They are developed in an attempt to explain or to provide a coherent "map of the territory," presumably so we may feel more confident that we know where we are and what we are doing. Hopefully, etiologic theories also shed light on the possible causes of BPD, which may lead to prevention or inform treatment decisions. At times, however, theories can provide a safe haven for the therapist who may not know how to treat someone but can at least take solace in explaining the pathology. Theories can enhance understanding and thus help us adopt a more compassionate view of our clients. However, sometimes theories can operate as conceptual blinders.

Some therapists become wedded to their theories or prefer to view causal factors from a unidimensional point of view. And, finally, some theorists describe their model in obscure or esoteric jargon such that only the "enlightened" can decipher what they mean.

I am going to suggest that what has come to be seen as borderline personality disorders cannot be understood in a simplistic way. These various types of psychopathology likely represent a common pathway or outcome for a multitude of different causes. In this chapter I shall very briefly review some theories of etiology. This will not be a comprehensive discussion; rather my intent is to offer some ideas that will have bearing on later material that is more directly related to treatment issues.

NEUROBIOLOGICAL FACTORS

Several theories have been put forth that shed light on the role of neurobiological factors in BPD. A brief discussion of some of these theories follows.

Temperamental Defects

Inborn (neuro-developmental) defects, especially those affecting brain structures/systems that play a role in emotional regulation (e.g., limbic system, hypothalamus, frontal cortex, serotonin, dopamine, and/or noradrenergic neurotransmitter systems), may lead to developmental problems in several ways.

Some children (destined to develop BPD) come into the world in a state of *extreme biologically based emotional sensitivity.* Thus, what otherwise might be normal experiences of discomfort or frustration could be experienced as overwhelmingly painful or traumatic. This infant or young child would, of course, experience considerable added distress if he/she is born into a chaotic, abusive, or non-nurturing family. Extreme sensitivity, overreactivity, and intense distress could contribute to inadequate ego development. Borderline personality disorder is five times more common among first degree relatives, which may suggest some genetic loading for this disorder (APA 1994).

Temperamentally difficult children are kids who often are hard to soothe and are a source of considerable stress, even for very capable, nurturing parents. Intense crying, crankiness, irritability, irregular sleep patterns, and difficulty being soothed may interfere with the quality of the parent-child bond. Inadequate attachment resulting from these difficult behaviors may interfere with ego development and the internalization of positive introjects.

Many theorists have hypothesized that one outcome of healthy parent-child interactions early in life is the gradual development of positive introjects. Introjects can be seen as a form of inner self-talk and deeply held beliefs; for example, "I am a decent person," "I deserve to find love with others," "It's O.K. for me to have feelings and needs." These inner beliefs reflect the messages the child receives from his/her parents in day-in, day-out interactions during the years of early childhood.

Some children are born with the vulnerability to develop certain Axis I disorders that have been shown to have rather strong genetic predispositions (e.g., bipolar and schizophrenic spectrum disorders). Thus, a contributing factor may be the emergence of these more neurobiologically based disorders, which can, at times, first arise symptomatically in childhood or adolescence.

Note: A number of authors suggest that approximately 10 percent of borderline patients come from intact families without evidence of severe early stress or trauma. It is important to consider that a number of our borderline patients, therefore, may not have had terrible childhoods or maltreatment, but rather have weak egos and exquisite sensitivity traceable to neurobiological deficits.

Neurobiological Deficits

Some people develop what appear to be borderline characteristics after sustaining neurological injuries (e.g., head injuries). In addition to cognitive difficulties, the most common emotional/behavioral consequences are impaired emotional controls (especially manifested as irritability and impulsivity). If these individuals were injured in late childhood, adolescence, or adulthood, they often have had the good fortune to have developed healthy relationships with others and to have developed a "self" prior to the injury. Thus, the clinical picture may look "borderline-like" (due primarily to the symptoms of emotional dyscontrol and impulsivity), but, on closer inspection, there is a higher level of development with regard to interpersonal relatedness and the self. This may distinguish this group from more classical borderline patients.

Recent years have seen increased emphasis placed on the role of psychological trauma in the pathogenesis of BPD (Essex, et al. 2002; Heim and Nemeroff 2002; Heim et al. 2000; Schore 2001; Teicher et al. 2002). One consequence of severely traumatic experiences (especially early in life) may be its impact on brain development. Much theorizing has come out of animal research (and some limited human studies) that focuses on two major classes of traumatic experience: (1) severe neglect and (2) intrusive events. Some general conclusions from these studies are addressed below.

Severe Neglect

Across a broad range of mammalian species, the impact of severe neglect appears to result in a rather predictable cluster of behavioral abnormalities as outlined below (Weiss and Kilts 1995).

- Significantly impaired affective controls manifested by low frustration tolerance, lability, and impulsive behavior

- A predominance of aggressive behavior

- When under stress, a tendency for self-mutilation (e.g., severely neglected monkeys will pull out their hair, bang their heads against cage walls, and, at times, bite off their fingers)

- A tendency to hyperingest alcohol (something most normal mammals do not do)

Intrusive Events

The second class of traumatic experience can be seen as intrusive events. These include physical abuse, sexual molestation, and severe emotional harshness (e.g., humiliation, shaming, extreme criticism). An important element in these experiences that elevates them to a *traumatic* level is a sense of utter powerlessness or helplessness.

In animal models, an *inescapable shock paradigm* has frequently been used. In these obnoxious experiments, animals are subjected to very painful electrical shocks, from which they are unable to escape. Initial attempts to mount a coping response or to escape, at some point, give way to a state of abject passivity. In a sense, the animals collapse and stop trying to escape.

This is accompanied by a number of physiological responses that are quite similar to those seen in humans suffering from major depression: sleep disturbances, appetite loss and weight loss, decreased libido, and elevations in glucocorticoids (adrenal stress hormones). In addition, these animals show evidence of a pronounced startle response and increased activation of the norepinephrine neurotransmitter system in the brain. Finally, there is evidence in both humans and animals of permanent structural changes in certain aspects of the limbic system (e.g., the hippocampus).

A critical point to emphasize is that, in many instances, these behavioral and neurobiologic changes last long after the stressful stimuli end. (In fact, they often last for a lifetime.) Thus, the implication is that, although a person may come into the world with an intact central nervous system, severe emotional trauma may play a role in dramatically altering brain development and functioning. This, of course, represents difficulties above and beyond the more purely psychological consequences of trauma.

TREATMENT IMPLICATIONS OF NEUROBIOLOGICAL IMPAIRMENT

What are the implications of considering neurobiological impairments in BPD? I believe they are threefold. First, this type of impairment may help to explain why certain psychotropic medications are effective in treating BPD and, hopefully, may guide the development of newer medications. A second implication is that this can help us understand some of the reasons why these disorders are so persistent and so difficult to treat. For many of our borderline clients, at least some part of their difficulties may be seen as rooted in abnormal neurobiology. As evidence accumulates revealing further biologic aspects of BPD, we may become able to point to these neurobiologic aspects in our efforts to persuade legislators and health care policy makers that these are "real" disorders. Often medical illnesses are seen as more "legitimate" if some abnormality can be seen on a lab test or C.T. scan.

There is a final implication. Keeping the biological piece of the picture in mind has helped me to maintain perspective. I have had moments with borderline clients when I wanted to shout "Just calm down!" or "Don't be so damned sensitive!" I find it easier to contain some of my own adverse reactions by remembering, "At some level, a part of their problem may be hard-wired into their nervous system . . . and to a degree, they can't help it." I do not mean to imply that neurobiological deficits are permanently set in concrete and not malleable. Nor do I want to suggest that borderline people have no responsibility for their behavior; ultimately they do. But appreciating the neurobiological component tells me what I'm up against and allows me to feel an extra measure of compassion.

ETIOLOGY: PSYCHOLOGICAL AND INTERPERSONAL FACTORS

Many theories that focus on the role of early traumatic experiences and other psychologically damaging events have been suggested in the pathogenesis of severe personality disorders. A comprehensive review of such theories is beyond the scope of this book. Rather, I would like to highlight briefly some common themes that emerge from the voluminous literature.

Recently, there has been a good deal of focus on the role of severe childhood trauma and its effect of derailing normal emotional development. Some authors suggest that the majority (90 percent) of people with BPD experienced severely traumatic events as youngsters (e.g., physical and sexual abuse, witnessing domestic violence) (Perry, Herman, et al. 1990; Zanarini 1996; Linehan 1993; Gabbard 1996a). What is interesting is that many borderline clients do not spontaneously report traumatic histories, although, as a rule, such data can be gleaned from very detailed historical inquiries (van der Kolk 1994).

Many of our borderline clients have lived through horrible experiences of physical, sexual, and emotional abuse. However, it seems likely that *single* traumatic events do not generally have such a profound effect as to completely derail personality development. What is more likely is that borderline people have experienced either recurrent traumas and/or have endured chronic, ongoing, psychologically noxious experiences (e.g., day-in, day-out rejection, harshness, brutality, severe neglect, and so forth). I would like to classify such noxious events into five classes.

Early Child-Parent Interactions (1)

The first class is the impact of seriously disturbed early child-parent interactions (especially during the first year of life). This can be traced to circumstances of nurture or fate (Masterson 1976). Sometimes mothers (and fathers), owing to their own severe psychopathology, are unwilling or unable to provide an adequate emotional connection with the infant. This may be due to a failure in empathy, as, for example, in a mother who is simply unable to sense her child's emotions and needs (what Masterson calls a "communicative mismatch"). Another example would be the immature, egocentric parent who is so profoundly self-centered that he/she is unable to give love to the child. A not infrequent event is the mother suffering from a severe post-partum depression. This mother may be emotionally mature and fully capable of providing appropriate love and nurturing under ordinary circumstances, but due to serious depressive symptoms she has become severely impaired, overwhelmed, and unavailable to her child.

Fate (2)

Fate plays a role in cases where babies have serious medical problems and must be hospitalized for prolonged periods of time (interrupting more normal parent-child bonding) or when a parent either becomes seriously ill or dies. It is widely believed that "good enough" nurturing is essential early in life to hasten the development of the ego. Extreme emotional sensitivity and other signs of significant ego impairment often are the consequences of major emotional deprivation in the earliest months of life.

Individuation Issues (3)

A number of aversive circumstances present in later stages of child development have also been posited as contributing to flawed personality development. Mahler, Pine, and Bergman (1975) have paid particular attention to factors occurring during the stages of separation-individuation. In particular, they hypothesize that many future borderline patients experience a significant lack of support for individuation. One version of this scenario, for example, may be seen when a mother clings to her baby and infantilizes the child while feeling anxious or threatened by the child's early attempts to separate and become an independent person. Kids need tremendous encouragement and support as they begin to take steps out into the "other than mother world" (Mahler 1975). When this support is absent or attempts to individuate are actually punished, arrested development is a common outcome. Presumably, the more natural blossoming of the self is impeded and ego development suffers. Such kids may become developmentally fixated at immature levels of both ego functioning and growth of the self.

Invalidating Environments (4)

Linehan speaks of the "invalidating environment" often seen in the borderline's family of origin (1993). This environment is characterized by the following behaviors: The child's communication of inner needs, beliefs, and feelings is often met by inappropriate, nonaccepting, and extreme reactions by parents (The child is punished, trivialized, dismissed, shamed, or disregarded.) Linehan believes that this experience has a profound negative effect on the development of internal affective controls. Additionally, it leaves the child mistrustful of his/her inner experience (and thus less able to acknowledge inner feelings and needs and less likely to experience them as legitimate or understandable).

Inadequate Parental Models (5)

Many parents of future BPD patients provide poor behavior models. They are often chaotic, impulsive, and extreme in their emotional reactions, and unable to help teach or model self-control, appropriate social behavior, and problem-solving skills.

Of course, these are just hypotheses, although they have received rather broad acceptance. Aside from academic speculation, what is *useful* to us in these theories? Since these kinds of life experiences probably characterize much of a borderline client's early life, it is especially important for therapists to be attuned to these issues and to offer something different to our patients, that is, corrective experiences.

Early life events may have the power to alter brain development, they certainly can result in bad memories, and, very importantly, they can have a profound effect on enduring cognitive schemas and world views. Many people who have been traumatized or abused as children develop deeply entrenched beliefs such as, "I am completely worthless," "I am unlovable," or "All I can ever expect from others is hurt and abandonment." These views (whether conscious or unconscious) are carried into all later life experiences and can markedly influence expectations and color perceptions in present-day, adult interactions. Such views contribute to an ongoing sense of bitterness, pessimism, and/or hopelessness. These are not just old wounds that still hurt, but are more a matter of the borderline patient's enduring beliefs about current realities and hopes for the future, which color ongoing perceptions of their world.

Beyond this, borderline people provoke others into strong reactions, in powerful ways. The result is thus not only a *history* of rejection, abuse, and abandonment, but also an *ongoing* series of similar experiences. We must keep in mind that almost everyone in the borderline patient's life has been provoked into counterattack, distancing, or rejection. (BPD clients also frequently recruit others into caretaker roles, which can repeat interaction patterns where the clients are treated as helpless infants.) Therapists are drawn into these kinds of roles, too, and must be on guard against them.

As we become sensitized to the nature and consequences of early hurtful experiences, we can become more attuned to and understand our own reactions to our clients, being especially cautious not to repeat interactions that are invalidating, overly harsh, attacking, overinfantilizing, or rejecting. The capacity to resist the urge to respond in such negative ways is one of the most important elements for successful treatment of people with severe personality disorders.

PART III

TREATMENT ISSUES

CHAPTER 3

Core Characteristics and Treatment Implications

Beyond the general characteristics associated with borderline personality disorders discussed in Chapter 1, there are a number of important clinical features that often become apparent as we initiate treatment with these clients. In this chapter I would like to further describe these clinical features and begin to discuss some general treatment issues. (In later chapters we will explore more specific intervention strategies.)

What follows is a discussion of seven important classes of behavioral characteristics.

1. Cognitive Dysfunctions

2. Loss of Temporal Perspective

3. Interpersonal Instability

4. Emotional Dysregulation

5. Intense Anger

6. Primitive Defenses

7. Ease of Regression

I hope this will be read as more than a description of symptoms; my intent is to highlight a number of critical behaviors, interactions, and dynamics common to this group of people. Some of these we simply observe; others we are drawn into during the course of treatment and experience in a more personal way. Although not all characteristics apply to every borderline patient, most clients manifest at least several of these features.

COGNITIVE DYSFUNCTIONS

In general, the style of cognition and information processing seen in borderline people is best described as reactive, impulsive, and nonreflective.

Reflective Thinking

The capacity to contain or modulate emotional responses, curb impulsivity, and behave in adaptive ways is very dependent on one's ability to hold action in check, and to *reflect* (what psychoanalysts refer to as "mentalization"). By reflecting I mean the following:

- To be able to assess situations carefully

- To perceive important elements of situations accurately (requiring adequate reality-testing skills)

- To plan actions that are likely to be adaptive, and

- To anticipate consequences

Under optimum conditions, this includes not only an assessment of external reality, but also an awareness of inner feelings, needs, and beliefs. (What Marsha Linehan calls the "wise mind" approach.) This internal cognitive activity allows one to choose behaviors (emotional expressions, problem-solving actions, interpersonal communications) that stand a better chance of being adaptive and are grounded in one's own feelings and needs.

Cognitive Paralysis

Taken to the extreme, cognitive reflection can result in paralysis and excessive inhibition. This is seen in many obsessional people who frequently get trapped in thinking, analyzing, and ruminating and cannot act. At the other extreme, an absence of reflective behavior leads to spontaneity (at best) or to impulsive, maladaptive reactions (at worst).

Impulsive Thinking

Many emotionally healthy people are prone to react in nonreflective, impulsive ways when in danger or under stress. (For example, if you are about to be run over by a bus, stopping in the street to carefully consider your options is not a good idea.) Under stress, many of us become more *reactive* and the behaviors that result are sometimes excessive or ultimately maladaptive. However, in general, neurotic and highly mature people do not succumb to extreme impulsivity, even during times of significant distress.

Borderline people, on the other hand, are quite prone to a much more maladaptive information-processing style. This can take the form of extreme black-and-white thinking, jumping to unrealistic conclusions, and a severe loss of a realistic perspective. It is an approach to thinking that has been referred to as "stimulus-bound," which describes the tendency to become so focused on the events of the moment that one loses perspective and awareness of historical antecedents or future consequences. Consider the following case example:

> **Case Example:** It had been a pleasant day. George had done everything just right to give his wife a splendid anniversary celebration, complete with flowers, dinner, and a special wine. During their romantic dinner, he received an urgent call from his supervisor at work and had to spend ten minutes on the phone. When he returned to the table, his wife, Laura, exploded at him, breaking a wineglass on the floor and calling him "a cold, uncaring son of a bitch." She had become intensely angry because of the phone call and had concluded "the bastard doesn't give a damn about me, leaving me here all alone." George was astonished by her reaction. He genuinely loves Laura, and had done a lot to make the day special for her and to let her know that it was special for him, too.

Here, we see a behavioral phenomenon common in borderline people. Laura became so intensely focused on the moment (i.e., "I'm all alone, George has been on the phone for what *feels* like forever, everyone is looking at me and wondering why he left me here") that she totally failed to consider all of the other data (i.e., the flowers, the fine restaurant, the special wine, his expressions of love, etc.). She became stimulus-bound and lost all perspective.

In all likelihood, Laura's reaction was determined by a number of factors including an extreme sensitivity to being alone or perceived abandonment, and poor emotional controls. A central part of her problem, however, can be seen as a breakdown in cognitive functioning. A more adaptive approach might have been for her to consider "I really don't like it when business calls interrupt our celebration. But George has been such a sweetheart today, and I know that he'll be back soon." This does not deny her uncomfortable feelings, but it does require the kind of thinking that helps people cope with daily frustrations and disappointments. Of course, sensitivity and poor emotional control are not seen exclusively in borderline people. Most people experience these kinds of feelings from time to time. But for lower-functioning people, maladaptive information processing can be pervasive. And, often, the inaccurate conclusions lead to intense or extreme overreactions.

Note: This cognitive style has nothing to do with intellectual level. I've treated people with doctorate degrees who exhibit this kind of behavior. In nonemotion-arousing situations (especially situations where there is predictability, structure, and little stress) intelligent borderline individuals can think clearly (sometimes well enough to get through medical school or to become the president of a corporation). But under even mild stress, clear thinking and reflective abilities tend to evaporate.

Cultivating the Pause

Helping borderline people develop more adaptive strategies for thinking and problem solving is a very important aspect of their treatment. It requires the patient to call on at least *momentary* impulse/emotional control; what some therapists call "cultivating the pause." During this pause, the person may be able to engage in an assessment of the situation and plan more appropriate responses. The specifics of this strategy will be discussed in detail in Chapter 4, "Fundamental Treatment Decisions."

LOSS OF TEMPORAL PERSPECTIVE

The ability to transcend a perception of the moment and to balance one's view of what is taking place with reference to the past and the future is an important aspect of cognitive processing (Kroll 1988). The notion of temporal perspective is related to the concept of stimulus-bound perceptions discussed above; but it also contains some important additional elements. Let's illustrate this with two case examples.

> **Case Example:** Arthur just got chewed out by his boss for a mistake he made in the latest budget report. He feels hurt, irritated with himself, and somewhat ashamed. Upon his return to his office, Arthur says to himself, "Well, I blew that. I can't believe I screwed it up—but I rarely make mistakes, I have a great track record with this company. I've received good performance evaluations and promotions. I know I'm not incompetent—I just made a really dumb mistake. Everybody makes mistakes sometimes. To err is human, isn't it?"

What we see here is Arthur's capacity to recall past events in his work life accurately. He is reality testing and reminding himself of the truth regarding his work performance. Calling forth memories of past positive experiences helps him to regain perspective and to partially disengage from the upsetting encounter with his boss. This sort of thinking is a major way that people "self-soothe."

Most borderline people in the midst of an emotional situation lose the capacity to draw on this kind of temporal perspective. They become engulfed in the moment and experience only hurt, despair, and other negative feelings. They are unable to call forth reassuring memories and images from other parts of their life. This contributes to the perception of an "all-bad" self. No wonder life is so hard for these people.

When borderline clients are in crisis, an important role for the therapist is to serve as an "auxiliary ego" and to do for them what they cannot do for themselves: reality test, reflect on past experiences, and regain a more realistic view of the self.

Case Example: In the aftermath of a rejection from her boyfriend, Kathy became very distraught and reacted by scratching and severely cutting her arms with a piece of broken glass. In her next therapy session she exclaimed, "Jim dumped me . . . now I have no one . . . absolutely no one in the world gives a damn about me!" The therapist replied, "Obviously it hurts a lot to feel rejected by Jim. I know he's meant a lot to you. But Kathy, let me ask you something . . . Is it completely true that absolutely no one in the world cares about you? How about Sara (one of her very close friends) and Tim (her brother)?"

Kathy says, "Well, yes they do care, but it's not the same!" Therapist, "I believe that . . . At the same time, I want to ask you, does it matter at all to know that Sara and Tim really do genuinely care about you?" Kathy, "Well, yes it does, I guess." (She calms down.)

In these moments, Kathy's view of her interpersonal world is especially bleak while she believes that she has no one who cares for her at all. She accepts this conclusion as a fact. It's true that she has had a bona fide loss that must be faced and grieved. But her loss of perspective has propelled her into overwhelming distress.

One of my clients once said to me: "John, you are like my memory. I count on you to remind me of things that I seem to forget at real emotional times." Providing this kind of memory is another function we perform for clients who lose their ability to remember other parts of their lives under stress.

Temporal Perspective and Devaluation of the Therapist

Two other manifestations of the loss of temporal perspective are worth noting. The first is seen in the common phenomenon where a patient rapidly shifts from a positive or idealized view of the relationship with the therapist into an angry devaluation. This is a striking and often disturbing reaction to encounter, especially for the novice therapist. I've had many occasions when I believed that I was being very supportive, caring, and nonjudgmental with a patient, and then I would be stung by a suddenly emerging, degrading devaluation, e.g., "You therapists are all alike . . . just a bunch of cold, money-hungry assholes!"

Although, I've never actually said this, my impulse has been to respond with, "Hey, wait a minute. I'm a nice guy. I've been like Mother Theresa with you. Don't you remember?" They probably would answer "No I don't." Because, at that moment, borderline clients *don't* remember. Once again, we see the borderline person's tendency to get locked into the perception and the emotion of the moment. (Often, times of intense devaluation are a response either to the client feeling misunderstood or rejected, or, conversely, feeling too close to the therapist, and needing something to create distance.) Therapists must tolerate such attacks, stand firm, try to understand what just happened, and, at some point, help the person to regain a more realistic perspective.

Temporal Perspective and Loss

Finally, if people are to adequately grieve losses, the ability to call forth past memories and images is important. When people mourn, an important element of the experience is to vividly recall memories of the lost person (painful as well as positive memories). This helps them accept and come to terms with the realities of their loss and to discover inner feelings and meanings associated with these painful events. Borderline people are often incapable of calling forth such memories and images, and thus may be significantly hampered in their attempts to work through major losses.

INTERPERSONAL INSTABILITY

So often the early life experiences of borderline clients were colored by tremendously harmful relationships. Destructiveness, abuse, harshness, neglect, and smothering can have a profound impact on emotional development, especially as this relates to the development of object relations. Object relations (an unfortunate term, in my view) refers to the *internalization of interpersonal experiences*. Day-in, day-out interactions early in life influence the development of internal cognitive schemas in a profound way. These schemas are deeply ingrained beliefs about the world (what happens and what to expect). Of particular significance are schemas that center around three issues:

- **What are people like?** (How have I been treated by others and, in general, what do I anticipate when I encounter new people?)

- **Who am I?** (What makes me tick, what matters to me, what are my most important needs?)

- **What is likely to happen if I begin to relate to another?** (e.g., Will I be treated decently? . . . Will I be used? . . . Will I be engulfed by the other? . . . Will I lose my self? . . . Will I be attacked? . . . Will I be abandoned?)

Core Schemas

These inner beliefs may continue for a lifetime and have a profound effect on day-to-day experiences. Schemas greatly influence and bias interpretations of ongoing experience (especially interpersonal interactions). If the dominant core belief is that, "Ultimately everyone hates me and abandons me," it is likely that many situations will be perceived (or misperceived) as involving rejections. People with such core beliefs are very likely to misread subtle social cues, facial expressions, and other behaviors and to jump to conclusions that verify their inner, rigidly held beliefs.

One marker of psychopathology is the degree to which core schemas can be modified by later life experiences. For example, people who were subjected to significant early mistreatment may be able to modify core schemas when later in life they develop a supportive relationship with a kind person or have a corrective experience with a caring therapist. More severely disturbed people, however, show extreme rigidity in their schemas, as if their beliefs are set in psychic concrete. In these instances, benign or even positive relationships fail to result in any fundamental alteration of the core beliefs. So a therapist might be tremendously supportive and genuinely caring, yet the client continues to believe "Sooner or later she will screw me just like everyone else has" or "Well, he looks concerned, but it's probably that phony, therapist façade. I know all he really wants to do is to get rid of me."

These negative, rigid schemas are an important source of interpersonal instability. For example, consider a scenario where the borderline client encounters a genuinely nice person. They become friends—or lovers. As the two of them spend time together and become closer, the borderline person continues to be as suspicious as at the onset of the relationship, questions the sincerity of the other's behavior, accuses the other of not really caring, and so forth. At some point, the other person loses patience and withdraws. He/she gets tired of never being trusted, of always being questioned or accused, and backs out of the relationship, because not only is it unrewarding, it is energy-draining. The client then concludes, "See, I was right. She/he never gave a damn about me." Therapists, of course, will be tested in similar ways by our borderline clients.

It's easy to feel frustrated when we try hard to be supportive and then encounter abusive criticism and other forms of attack from our clients. But it must be kept in mind that the borderline person's ongoing misperceptions are very likely to:

- Make sense, if we can come to understand the context of their early life experiences, and

- Serve an adaptive function—to keep the person on guard and alert to possible hurtful interactions. (Sensitivity to and vigilance towards potential noxious interactions can keep these borderline people from getting hurt again. Unfortunately, there are many mis-reads and false alarms.)

The Therapist's Ability to Tolerate Patients' Distortions

As previously stated, one of the most important factors for successful treatment of borderline cases is the therapist's ability to tolerate the patient's distorted perceptions about the relationship and to endure degrading accusations. The therapist's persistence in resisting the urge to reject the patient may be the only chance the person will ever have to modify very negative cognitive schemas.

Many borderline patients are very dependent people. Their interactions are dominated by extreme neediness and clinging behaviors. Often this is accompanied by a significant degree of egocentricity, such that when they enter relationships, they demand a lot, but are much less capable of giving to the other person. This can be seen in behavior that many label as selfish, greedy, manipulative, jealous, and demanding. A deficit in empathy for the other may also be a part of this constellation of behaviors.

Although many borderline people attract others and become involved in intimate relationships, most of the time the one-sided nature of their relating creates problems. Sooner or later, the other person begins to tire of giving a lot and getting little in return. If the other is not immediately available to meet the borderline individual's needs, he/she may encounter an intense temper tantrum, sullen pouting, or desperate clinginess. Rather than invoking more caring and deeper closeness, these behaviors provoke the other into withdrawal or arguing, and contribute to a further deterioration of the relationship. Demands for more contact escalate and can result in disastrous outcomes (e.g., manipulative suicidal gestures or physical violence).

This neediness is often experienced in the context of psychotherapy, such as when the patient has difficulty stopping when the session is over, or makes numerous between-session phone calls. This behavior, in turn, frequently evokes strong counter-transference reactions in the therapist (e.g., feeling overwhelmed by the patient's demands, or feeling worn-out, burned-out, and frustrated because it seems as if the client has an insatiable need for support, nurturing, and caretaking). Striking a balance between firm, realistic limit setting and appropriate availability is tricky, and crucial to successful outcomes. Chapter 7 focuses on this aspect of therapy in greater detail in the section entitled "Specific Expectations, Rules, and the Contract."

Fear of Engulfment

Other borderline patients become terrified in situations where there is intimacy or emotional closeness. (This is more characteristic of lower-level borderline pathology and of schizoid and schizotypal disorders.) Thus, although these borderline people may seek out others to some degree, if the other gets too close, it frightens them. Often this fear leads to withdrawal or to behaviors that create interpersonal distance. (One such common and powerful behavior is intense explosions of anger—which, naturally, causes most people to back away.)

Some theorists have suggested that this anxiety regarding intimacy or closeness is associated with primitive fears of being engulfed by or merged with the other. Borderline clients will talk about fears of losing their self (sometimes described as fear of disintegration, becoming invisible, or being swallowed by the other). Additionally, so many of these people were badly abused children; it makes a good deal of sense that they fear closeness. Early in their lives, the people they were closest to hurt them terribly.

These clients are so terrified of closeness that we need to be very sensitive to their terror, respecting their needs for boundaries and separateness. There are times when even a benign, but empathic comment by the therapist may be experienced, at least unconsciously, by the patient as "getting too close."

Dependency Versus Fear of Intimacy

A number of borderline clients exhibit both features: tremendous dependency/neediness *and* fear of closeness. In some situations, they are motivated by their hunger for human contact and will seek out connections. However, this may quickly be replaced by a shift into the fear of closeness and by desperate attempts to create distance. This kind of contradictory behavior is often extremely perplexing to others who at first receive "come closer" signals and then "back off messages." It can be a terribly confusing experience, and is a common trigger for intense interpersonal friction and dramatic rejections.

Negotiating the fine line between "too close" and "too distant" is difficult, but *essential* in the therapeutic relationship. Borderline clients can, in powerful ways, entice therapists into inappropriate closeness. I have often felt a strong urge to hold or hug BPD patients as I witnessed their very intense emotional suffering (although such physical contact is strongly contraindicated). It's hard to restrain such a natural human response to provide this kind of comfort to someone in such pain. The temptation is strong to extend therapy time or to respond to many between-session phone calls. Equally powerful is the urge to back off or even counterattack when the client engages in threatening behavior or abusive devaluation.

I think this fine-tuning of appropriate engagement and distance is expressed well in the following story:

> "A number of porcupines huddled together for warmth on a cold day in winter; but as they began to prick one another with their quills, they were obliged to disperse. However the cold drove them together again, when just the same thing happened. At last, after many turns of huddling and dispersing, they discovered that they would be best off by remaining a little distance from one another."
>
> —Arthur Schopenhauer

Obnoxious Behaviors and Extreme Solutions

Several other aspects of borderline interpersonal relationships set the stage for considerable turmoil and instability. The first is *obnoxious interpersonal behavior*. In the heat of an argument, borderline patients frequently do and/or say things that wound deeply or are very hard to forgive. For example, a patient of mine had a borderline mother who flew into a rage and punished my client by forcing her to watch while she cut the feet off my client's pet duck. Another all too common obnoxious behavior is to use especially degrading words during arguments. A client once told me that he had called his girlfriend "a sack of shit and a stinking whore." Understandably, most people find it hard to forget or forgive such intense, degrading expressions of anger.

Another class of behaviors that I call *extreme solutions* can also destabilize relationships. Extreme solutions are common occurrences in borderline marriages or other intimate relationships. This behavior manifests in the heat of an argument, when one person threatens to completely end the entire relationship with statements like, "I'm just going to get a divorce!" or "It's all over. You can kiss *this* marriage good-bye!" Even if the couple ultimately "make up," this can and does have a marked impact on the degree of trust present in a relationship. Higher-functioning people certainly can become quite angry, but they are less prone to make such extreme statements.

These kinds of extreme solution reactions are also seen in therapy at the end of a difficult session; e.g., a BPD patient may storm out of the office exclaiming "You don't give a damn about me. You never did. Screw you. I'm never coming back."

Unrealistic Expectations and Intolerance for Disillusionment

A final element of interpersonal instability in the borderline patient is an intolerance for disillusionment. Many of these people are desperately needy and constantly on the lookout for the perfect spouse (or therapist or the perfect psychiatric medication) while engaging in magical thinking about eliminating their loneliness, emptiness, depression, and so forth. These unrealistic expectations are likely tied to infantile neediness and a reliance on magical thinking. One result is they enter relationships rapidly with inflated hopes and idealize the other. This quickly gives way to tremendous disappointment when the lover, friend, or therapist fails to provide magical solutions. The result can be bitter disappointment and, often, a radical shift from idealization to devaluation. It is not rare for a therapist to hear in one session "You are the best, most competent therapist I've ever seen" and in the next session to hear "You are an uncaring bastard"! Not exactly the kind of comment that therapists like to bask in.

Impulsive, extreme solutions and radical shifts from idealization to devaluation are very difficult for most people to understand or to endure, and those behaviors certainly contribute to the intense turmoil that characterizes so many borderline relationships. Good therapists certainly do not enjoy these experiences, but they can at least *understand* them. Once again, the willingness and ability to absorb this erratic behavior and to maintain appropriate availability is a key to therapeutic success.

EMOTIONAL DYSREGULATION

Emotional dysregulation is possibly the most central feature of borderline-level pathology. This is revealed in intense, poorly modulated expressions of emotions; reactions that are markedly maladaptive and that often end up creating serious problems in relationships. Related to this is low frustration tolerance. Minor stresses are experienced as overwhelming and borderline people often insist that they "can't stand" inner distressing feelings.

BPD clients have a restricted range of affective tolerance. Most times, when they encounter upsetting and painful events, only two options seem available to them; which is not to imply that they have or make conscious choices about these styles of reaction. The first option is a profound loss of control (i.e., dyscontrol). The second is to go to any lengths to avoid awareness of inner dysphoria (i.e., the use of primitive defenses). To experience and express emotions in a mature, well-modulated way is very difficult for them. This is a serious problem because it leaves the borderline individual unable to engage in what, for most of us, is the major avenue for emotional healing. When people encounter difficult and painful times, for healing to take place it seems to be necessary to face the truth of inner emotions, to understand them, to express them in appropriate ways, to validate the experience, to talk about inner experiences, and to share one's pain, to a greater or lesser degree, with another.

Emotional dysregulation is often the reason that borderline people seek treatment. They may externalize blame (e.g., "It's not my fault . . . That asshole boss is harassing me"), but on some level, most feel an overwhelming sense of being "out of control."

Intense emotional expression is not easy for most people to tolerate. Inevitably the borderline individual's behavior takes a toll on important relationships. Almost always, our clients will have experienced two kinds of reactions from others when they have lost control. The first occurs when strong emotions are provoked in the other person (e.g., counterattacks, accusations, intense criticism and verbal put-downs, interpersonal violence). The second occurs when people withdraw. Such strong feelings can be frightening and many people want no part of such a volatile relationship. Borderline people are then expelled from school, fired from jobs, rejected by lovers, or disowned by their own parents (or children). They end up burning many bridges as they move through life.

One very important and probably unique service therapists can offer their borderline clients is to act as an emotional shock absorber, receiving and containing emotional outbursts without being goaded into either counterattack or withdrawal. Believe it, this is often very hard to do. It is, however, critical (along with other strategies for reducing emotional dyscontrol that will be described later) because this kind of "neutral" receptivity can provide a powerful stabilizing force in the lives of our borderline clients.

INTENSE ANGER

One of the most common behaviors seen in people with severe personality disorders is *anger*. A lot of suffering is internal and private. However, anger is usually expressed in the interpersonal arena and is hard to ignore. Not only is this a pervasive characteristic, it is also a behavior that results in a good deal of ongoing interpersonal friction and countertransference difficulties. The phenomenon of borderline anger is quite complex and deserves special attention.

The anger expressed by borderline patients often is very intense, and may have a raw or primitive edge to it. It can take the form of temper tantrums, irritability, biting sarcasm, devaluation, vicious verbal attacks, or violence. One way to understand this is to view it as a symptom of emotional dysregulation and poor impulse control. And, certainly, this accounts for some of the anger that is exhibited, but other dimensions are also important to keep in mind.

A sense of profound powerlessness is a frequent experience for borderline people. In many instances, you will see outbursts of anger following on the heels of moments of intensely felt vulnerability, helplessness, or shame. It may be that anger serves to re-establish some sense of control or a defense against powerlessness and vulnerability. Not only is this seen in the form of transient expressions of anger; it is also manifested in the following ways.

Some borderline people get locked into a stance of extreme stubbornness. They may decide to battle others (or organizations) over certain issues that have to do with what they see as important principles. Often, this takes the form of an insistence that matters must be made fair or right. This can lead to a relentless struggle, often against impossible odds. Common wisdom suggests that people should choose their battles carefully. Sometimes, it is clear that pursuing certain conflicts will result in great personal suffering, and little likelihood of a positive outcome. For some borderline people the battle becomes a consuming mission; they insist that they must fight for what is right or to win, regardless of the personal costs. At times, this contains an element of revenge. To outsiders such behaviors clearly appear to be highly self-destructive. However, we must appreciate that, for the clients, the personal experiences involve a desperate attempt to maintain some sense of power.

Another common dynamic is to see anger emerge at times when the patient is beginning to feel too close to another person. As mentioned earlier, the issue of inter-personal closeness and neediness is often highly ambivalent. As the person senses the growth of greater closeness or intimacy, on some level this provokes intense anxiety. Becoming angry, abusive, or devaluing generally is an effective strategy for creating interpersonal distance; most people are likely to back off. This certainly happens in therapy. It may occur at moments where the client has just expressed strong feelings of neediness, or when the therapist has made an especially empathic or kind remark. This can be a perplexing and disturbing experience for a novice therapist. Unless the under-lying dynamic is understood, it seems to make little sense to encounter a touching moment and then suddenly feel a blast of anger coming from the client.

Another reason that anger may emerge is that it can serve as a "test" of the therapist. This perspective suggests that the patient acts in an angry way in order to see how the therapist will react. In typical interpersonal situations, almost everyone reacts to displays of intense anger either by withdrawing or by counterattack. In all likelihood, this has been the recurrent paradigmatic experience in borderline people's lives. If the therapist can resist the impulse to respond in these ways, and maintain a solid, noncritical, nonabandoning stance, in a sense he/she has passed the test; the therapist is then seen as "safe." It is important to be clear that this "testing" is almost never a conscious or deliberate choice; rather it is done in an automatic and largely unconscious way.

Finally, quite often anger arises naturally in response to experiences that have been significantly hurtful to the client. These situations include current events where the person has been used, abused, or in other ways hurt by others. It includes expressions of anger that are in response to recollections of past hurtful experiences. And, certainly it can be seen as a reaction to the therapist's behavior (e.g., empathic failures, being late for sessions, etc.). In each of these instances the client's anger may erupt in what appears to be overly intense or maladaptive ways, but it is very important to accept that the anger and underlying hurt are often entirely appropriate and understandable. Most of these people have been terribly hurt. They have a right to strong feelings about what they have experienced. Many borderline clients were not allowed to express feelings and needs as children, and expressions of anger in the present may represent a developmental advance. It's important to understand this as growth of the self, not pathology.

Too often the borderline's anger is reacted to in a very disparaging way. It is very important that therapists try to understand the dynamics behind the behavior. Ultimately, we want to help our clients to develop more mature and adaptive ways to express anger. We also want to help them to find ways to feel less vulnerable, and more capable of expressing their legitimate feelings and needs.

PRIMITIVE DEFENSES: SOLUTIONS THAT BACKFIRE

When therapists hear from their borderline clients that they are feeling anxious, or depressed, or empty, it is important to consider that although the words used to describe inner feelings certainly sound familiar, in some fundamental ways they are not. With BPD, these emotional states frequently go far beyond the level of suffering experienced by higher-functioning personalities. It has become clear to me, especially in listening carefully to intelligent, articulate BPD patients, that their inner pain is often qualitatively different, and quantitatively more pronounced than most of us neurotics could ever imagine. Probably, this is due in part to the primitive, raw nature of their anguish. These people don't just suffer ordinary anxiety. Many times their anxiety is related to tremendous fears of personality disintegration (presently experienced as an intense fear of going crazy). Their sadness includes deep-seated convictions that they are utterly worthless. And emotions of loneliness and emptiness are often experienced as completely engulfing, inescapable, and painful to bear. Although such feelings may be intermittent, they have likely persisted for decades.

This intense and primitive suffering was captured in a recurring dream reported to me by a borderline patient. In the dream she is completely alone in deep space. It is utterly dark and isolated. The only thing in sight is a faint triangle in the distance. The triangular shape moves towards her slowly as she floats in darkness and silence. Eventually, after a long period of time, the triangle gets close enough so that she can begin to discern particular features. After a few more minutes, it becomes clear to her that each side of the triangle is composed of human faces. And each face is screaming out in agony, although she cannot hear their cries. She always awakens in a cold sweat.

Life stresses, especially interpersonal rejections and loneliness, often provoke a welling up of these desperate states of panic and despair, and call forth echoes of past experiences of abuse, neglect, contempt, disgust, and the awareness of having been hated by important others. The borderline person's weak ego defenses and diminished capacity for self-soothing only exacerbate matters further. The result is that they are frequently and recurrently either overwhelmed emotionally or hovering on the edge.

The reason I have belabored this point is to underscore the fact that the therapist must be able to appreciate the nature of their suffering in order to understand why they resort to what appears to be extremely maladaptive defenses. *All* of the defenses discussed below, on some level (despite their maladaptive consequences) *reduce emotional pain*, and to that extent are egosyntonic. When anyone tells borderline patients that their behavior is inappropriate or "sick," there is the great likelihood that they will not only feel criticized, they will also feel profoundly misunderstood.

I want to be absolutely clear that the defenses under discussion are extremely maladaptive and must be dealt with in treatment. But the successful therapist must have an appreciation of why these defenses are employed—before attempting to interfere with defensive behavior. This is quite different than treating neurotics. One of the cornerstones of psychodynamic therapy with neurotic clients is to work towards reducing the overuse of defenses. Most of the time, this is helpful because neurotics usually have adequate ego strength to loosen their defenses. They eventually discover that they are able to experience inner feelings more fully, and this leads to a greater sense of self and aliveness. Borderline patients, however, are significantly more vulnerable to being overwhelmed, and aggressive dismantling of their defenses can precipitate severe decompensation.

Impulsive Actions

The primary defense against the awareness of painful inner feelings, impulses, and needs, for borderlines clients, is *action*. As these people begin to experience distressing emotions, they quickly fly into actions that serve to distract them from the awareness of inner pain. Almost never is this done as a conscious act. It is impulsive. If asked, "Why did you do this?" many patients will honestly answer, "I don't know why." This class of defenses is often referred to as *acting out*. It includes the following behaviors:

- Provoking conflict, arguments, and fights with others

- Thrill seeking or engagement in dangerous activities (e.g., driving a speeding car on curving mountain roads; shoplifting)

- Temper tantrums, destructiveness, and violence (e.g., smashing dishes, torturing animals)

- Rampant promiscuity

- Excessive masturbation

- Binge eating with or without purging

- Self-mutilation (e.g., burning self, wrist slashing, drinking scalding water)

- Excessive abuse of alcohol and other substances

From an outsider's perspective, these behaviors appear to be very maladaptive and self-defeating. However, the borderline patient, *in the moment,* primarily experiences a sense of relief. And in the aftermath, there is a remarkable amount of denial about how self-defeating the behaviors were.

Denial

This brings us to a second common defense: *denial.* Everyone engages in occasional or mild levels of denial or minimization. However, the denial seen in borderline patients can be profound. In particular, there is denial regarding the consequences of their own chaotic and self-destructive behavior. Despite the presence of well-developed intellectual abilities in some BPD clients, borderline people are often remarkably oblivious to the impact of their erratic behavior.

Splitting

A third defense that has been written about extensively in the borderline literature is *splitting,* which is similar to categorical thinking or overgeneralizing. This is a cognitive operation in which the person (usually at times of emotional distress) tends to perceive reality in a global, black-or-white fashion. Typically, this emerges in the form of overgeneralized conclusions about others or one's self. (The other or the self is seen as either all-good or all-bad.) This can be viewed as a mistake in thinking or as a "cognitive distortion." It also can be appreciated as a way that humans process information and try to make sense of complex situations. This form of categorical thinking is characteristic of young children (and thus can be seen as a manifestation of immature cognitive functioning). It is also a common phenomenon when people are confronted with imminent danger. There is something profoundly adaptive in the mind's ability to rapidly appraise a situation and assign an immediate label of "good" or "not good" . . . "safe" or "dangerous." It has great survival value. This is what we do when a bus veering out of control is about to run over us. Get out of harm's way, and think about the details later.

Many people also jump to overgeneralized conclusions when in the midst of a lot of emotional turmoil, or when they need to form an opinion and little data is available. A final way to view splitting is that it is a way that people impose some kind of coherence on situations that otherwise might be impossible to understand. Some authors have suggested that splitting is a defense against collapse into the more disturbing state of confusion.

Thus, splitting is not unique to borderline clients, although it certainly occurs more frequently within this group. Often, as treatment progresses, the therapist may notice a decrease in splitting and evidence of an increased ability to consider complexities and "shades of gray." Let's consider some examples of increases in this ability:

> "I got pretty irritated with her, but I also know that she's put up with a lot of shit from me, and basically she has a good heart."

> "I felt disappointed in myself, but not completely worthless. I know that I'm really a pretty decent person, but sometimes I act like a jerk."

Self-Attack

Self-attack (in the form of self-criticism, devaluating, or physical harm) may be traced to numerous sources. Certainly it is often a manifestation of chronically low self-esteem and a deeply damaged self. It may also be seen as a type of defensive operation that analysts have traditionally called "changing passive-to-active." It works like this:

The person (sometimes consciously, but more often unconsciously) anticipates rejection, devaluation, or harshness from another. Rather than passively wait for the blow to come, he/she will fly into ruthless self-criticism and devaluation. Presumably, by doing it first, it reduces the likelihood that the other person will initiate an attack. This defense is often seen a moment or two after the client either has been assertive or has experienced vulnerability (e.g., by expressing needs or feelings; especially emotions accompanied by shame). (See Nathanson 1992.)

Projective Identification

The last defense to be discussed is *projective identification*. This is one of the more complicated defenses and it is also rather hard to grasp. It involves not only internal (intrapsychic) defenses, but also an interpersonal interaction. Presumably, this defensive operation begins with some experience of inner emotion (e.g., anger) that distresses the patient, who at this point has little conscious awareness of the emotion beyond feeling a vague uneasiness. This dis-ease motivates the patient to engage another person in an interaction that is generally provocative. In either obvious or incredibly subtle ways the borderline person does something, says something, or even simply looks at the other person in such a way that it provokes some strong response from the other. For example, the other person may become quite angry. The theory holds that the anger thus evoked in the other person *reassures the borderline client*, "I'm not the angry one; *he* is" and thus there is far less likelihood that the client will become aware of his own inner anger.

This is the traditional psychodynamic way of understanding projective identification: where the goal is to disavow one's inner emotions and, in a sense, project them onto the other person, who then acts them out. Whether or not you agree with this dynamic interpretation, the fact remains that borderline people do have an uncanny ability to provoke strong reactions in others. Whether this is purely defensive, or simply a maladaptive style of relating with others, is an open question. The major point regarding projective identification is that successful therapists must learn how to not take the bait. That is, they do not allow themselves to be provoked.

One final comment about defenses and defensive behaviors is in order here. It is a kind of mantra for me when I am doing psychotherapy. *Always remember, people defend because they are afraid.*

EASE OF REGRESSION

The term *regression* has a number of meanings ranging from the "get wild and crazy" disinhibition seen at parties, to the profound regression seen in severely psychotic individuals. One useful distinction has been to consider some forms of regression as "in the service of the ego." This refers to a potentially healthy, adaptive regression; the type of regression that results in relaxed defenses, more fluid thinking (including thought processes that can be viewed as creative or playful), and an increased openness to both external events and inner experience (e.g., feelings, images, intuition, etc.). It is "in the service of the ego," in that it aids adaptation, emotional healing, growth, and self-expression.

The capacity to regress in a healthy way can certainly be an asset and is a reflection of good ego strength. In mature people facing painful life challenges, one way regression "serves" the ego is by allowing them to become less guarded and open up to inner feelings. This is a crucial element in the process of mourning and the working through of very difficult life experiences. As stated earlier, rigidity and over-defensiveness are central problems for those deemed neurotic. The psychological gritting of teeth can present major problems for neurotic individuals who try their best to cope with difficult circumstances. In fact, techniques designed to *foster regression* are a central feature of treating neurotic clients. Helping clients open up to inner pain is often necessary (when it feels safe enough and when there is adequate rapport). Furthermore, the majority of books on psychotherapeutic technique have focused primarily on intervention strategies that do just that: open up, explore, and encourage increased access to inner experiences.

However, and this cannot be overstated, such *expressive or uncovering techniques can be the*

The writer James Joyce, so the story goes, took his severely disturbed daughter to see Carl Jung. After a two-hour consultation, Dr. Jung spoke with Joyce and informed him that his daughter had a psychotic illness. As he explained the symptoms of disordered and loose thinking and poor reality testing, the author commented, "Dr. Jung . . . you seem to be describing me too . . . especially when I am writing."

Dr. Jung replied, "It is like this metaphor . . . when you go to the river, you dip into the waters and drink. When your daughter goes to the river, she bends over, falls in, sinks to the bottom, and drowns."

Regression can quench thirst, or conversely, it can engulf and drown. It all depends on how sturdy a person is.

undoing of more fragile patients. An important, defining characteristic of BPD clients is the ease with which they regress; i.e., they are easily provoked into marked and very maladaptive states of regression. The results can be increased suffering, chaos, and therapeutic failure. In fact, those recorded cases of psychotherapeutic casualties are often traced to a therapist who unintentionally did something that provoked severe regression. As one of my professors at Baylor used to say, "These folks have one foot in catastrophe and the other on a banana-peel." Let's see what common factors can trigger this kind of maladaptive regression.

Factors That Promote Regression

1. **Lack of structure:** In highly predictable, familiar, and nonemotional settings, the absence of arousing stimuli and the presence of external structure can have a profound stabilizing effect on borderline people. In these circumstances, many may appear to function rather well. In sharp contrast, unfamiliar and unstructured circumstances can erode the borderline person's inner sense of control and stability; and marked regression can occur.

    The psychotherapy setting can provide a considerable amount of structure that helps the client develop or maintain better emotional containment and stability. Specifically, the following elements have been found to help provide the needed structure: clear, straightforward, and honest communications with the client, starting and stopping sessions on time, always charging for sessions, establishing contracts regarding treatment, limiting between-session telephone contacts, and *always* maintaining a strictly professional relationship (i.e., absolutely avoiding extra-therapy contacts, social, sexual, and business relationships, etc.).

    It is common for therapeutic disasters to unfold in the wake of lax boundaries (e.g., repeated sessions that extend beyond the agreed-upon time, numerous between-session phone calls, etc.).

    Therapists who faithfully maintain appropriate boundaries and structure may be accused by borderline clients of being "rigid," but in the long run are likely to be viewed as solid, safe, and reliable. These clients need an island of stability and the therapy (and the relationship with the therapist) can do much to provide this kind of anchor.

2. **Encouraging the exploration of dreams, fantasies, images, traumatic early memories, etc. The use of free association:** Ordinarily, these are the royal roads to one's inner life, but they are risky in the treatment of BPD. (Note: I do not mean to imply that therapists should never discuss these issues with borderline patients, but they should be aware that such discussion can undermine stability and promote regression.)

3. **"Uncovering" techniques:** (Also referred to as interventions designed to increase insight.) This includes the use of Gestalt techniques (and other evocative approaches such as guided imagery or hypnosis), intense probing,

and interpretation and confrontation of resistances. This issue is addressed in more detail in Chapter 4, "Fundamental Treatment Decisions."

4. **Frequent sessions:** Generally, frequent sessions tend to intensify emotional experience and may create conditions where regression takes place. (It should be noted that there are exceptions to this; at times of severe stress more frequent sessions may be helpful and necessary although the clinician should be cautious and watchful for signs of regression.)

5. **Prolonged silence and/or marked inactivity by the therapist:** These behaviors often increase anxiety and provoke regression.

6. **Primary gratification:** This term refers to therapist behaviors that presumably are aimed at providing direct gratification of a client's impulses, wants, or needs. Examples include *inappropriately* reducing professional fees, giving the client money or presents, physical contact (e.g., hugging, holding, sexual intimacy, etc.).

7. **Prolonged hospitalizations:** Brief hospitalizations are often necessary, especially at times of severe regression or when clients are judged to be very suicidal. The hospital can provide behavioral controls, structure, more intense crisis intervention, and more aggressive pharmacologic treatment. However, the hospital can also serve as an escape from ordinary life; a place to hide out and regress. This is much more likely to occur if the length of stay is either indefinite or prolonged. For this reason, many psychiatric hospitals tell borderline clients upon admission that the stay will be short (often only a few days) with a focus on achieving better emotional stability and a quick return to their normal living situation. It is also quite common practice that the outpatient therapist does not do inpatient treatment. A colleague provides the hospital-based treatment and the patient returns to the outpatient therapist upon discharge.

Hippocrates urged physicians, above all else, "Do no harm." An important cornerstone in the treatment of BPD is to do no harm by avoiding circumstances that foster regression.

CHAPTER 4

Fundamental Treatment Decisions

Before beginning a discussion of specific treatment strategies and interventions, it is important to consider some issues that I refer to as *fundamental treatment decisions*.

All psychotherapies rest on the bedrock of a solid, trusting, and compassionate relationship. A successful therapist must provide the critical ingredients of a good therapeutic relationship. At the heart of this is the capacity for empathy and a deep respect for our clients.

Beyond these essential features, psychotherapies differ considerably. However, one useful way to describe basic treatment approaches is to see them as taking one of two major paths: insight-oriented therapy or stabilizing interventions. Each pathway is characterized by particular techniques and interventions, but each is primarily defined by its overarching goal or objective.

INSIGHT-ORIENTED THERAPY

Pathway number one generally has been referred to as expressive, exploratory, uncovering, or insight-oriented psychotherapy. Its goal is to facilitate a process that helps the client to increase his/her awareness of inner experiences (e.g., awareness of needs, longings, feelings, and uniquely felt personal meanings, values, and beliefs). This may also include approaches designed to increase understanding (e.g., coming to know more about one's behaviors, making sense of past experiences, getting clear about inner truths). Techniques and interventions in this vein operate to heighten and intensify experience. They elicit responses, invite reflection, and encourage openness.

Such techniques are not inherently good or bad; it all depends. If these interventions take place prematurely with a constricted, inhibited, neurotic client, the fear of intense emotions or the experience of shame and vulnerability may lead to a hasty departure from treatment. However, well timed and balanced with sensitivity and care, these approaches may be the critical ingredient in treating the overdefended, very rigid neurotic. Conversely, expressive approaches are frequently risky with people who have marginal ego functioning. It may surely "open them up," but open them up to volcanic emotions and internal chaos.

STABILIZING INTERVENTIONS

Only with caution lift the lid on the id of the kid.

—Harry Wilmer

Pathway number two is the road to containment. Strategies here aim to decrease arousal, foster affective stabilization, and improve adaptive self-control. In a sense, the treatment is aimed at shoring up and strengthening a frail ego. This approach has often been called *supportive psychotherapy*, although this term may not be the best to describe such treatment. All psychotherapy is (or should be) supportive. And all too often, the concept of supportive therapy brings to mind images of hand-holding or baby-sitting. (Ultimately, successful treatments of BPD aim to avoid infantilization, and strive to empower and foster growth and autonomy.) I prefer to call these approaches *stabilizing interventions*. All techniques subsumed under this general heading are designed to improve ego functioning (to enhance emotional control, improve thinking and problem solving, and increase reality testing), and to foster the development of more adaptive coping strategies. In part, this also requires an active avoidance of interventions that promote regression or heighten arousal.

To take this out of the abstract realm and make it more concrete, I will take a brief look at the major interventions therapists commonly employ to achieve these two rather different objectives. A more detailed presentation of stabilizing interventions will follow in Chapter 8.

Expressive-Exploratory Interventions: To Increase Awareness and Heighten/Intensify Experiencing

Let's keep in mind that the following kinds of questions, probes, and comments often pervade many therapy sessions. These are the kinds of interventions most therapist are trained to provide.

1. **Clarification Questions:** These are designed to evoke more material.

   "Please tell me more about that."

   "I'm not clear about what you said. Could you please describe it in more detail?"

   "Let me check this out (rephrase or repeat client's remarks, then . . .) Is that right? Can you tell me more?"

2. **Confronting "Derivatives":** Clients often leak affective cues that signal the therapist that "a chord has just been struck." The inner emotion may or may not have registered at a conscious level. By confronting derivatives (the outward manifestations, such as a change in facial expression, vocal tone, altered rate of breathing, a sad look in the eyes) the therapist can often promote not only increased awareness, but such interventions may, in a powerful way, intensify the experience of the feeling in the moment.

   "Susan, as you were talking, I saw a change come over your face. What did you notice?"

   "All of a sudden, Bob, your eyes looked very sad. Are you aware of that?"

   "You look tense right now, Larry . . . What's going through your mind?"

3. **Probing:** Direct inquiries about inner feelings or thoughts.

   "Jill . . . What are you feeling right this moment?"

   "I wonder if there is more to it than that . . . Reflect on this a bit, Lucy . . . What else is going through your mind? . . . What else do you notice?"

4. **Dealing with Resistances:** Active interventions that attempt to counter and to reduce defensiveness in the moment.

   Client: I was pretty upset, but really, it wasn't that big a deal.

   Therapist: It wasn't a big deal? As you told me about this, I heard a lot of intensity in your voice.

   Client: Well, I guess I was pretty upset.

   Therapist: Pretty upset?

   Client: Well, really upset. It did get to me a lot!

   Client: Well, that's how a wife is supposed to feel when her husband leaves her. Right?

   Therapist: How *a wife* is supposed to feel? This was *your* marriage, *your* husband . . . How do *you* feel?

   Client: I feel awful.

In these examples, the therapist moves the client from a state of overcontrol into a more authentic experience of inner feelings.

5.   **Interpretive Comments:**

"I wonder if you were feeling a strong sense of loneliness and neediness: What do you think?"

"Could it be that you were feeling furious with him for making that comment?"

"Maybe it's hard for you to let yourself get too close to other people."

If interpretations accurately capture an experience, they often operate to turn up the volume of underlying emotions.

Stabilizing Interventions: To Decrease Arousal

Note: It is important to emphasize that the following interventions (strategies 1 through 3) are destined to fail unless the client first feels truly heard and his/her feelings are validated.

1.   **Challenging Distortions:** Actively confronting inaccurate, global, or arbitrary conclusions and encouraging the client to "explore the facts."

Client (to the therapist): You don't give a damn about me. You never have and I hate your guts. You're like all the other men I've known. Just a bunch of phony bullshit and no heart!

Therapist: I can see you are really mad at me. And maybe there's a good reason. I want to talk to you about it. But first, I want to encourage you to think about what you just said—that I don't give a damn about you. During the time you've been in therapy with me, have there been any times when it seemed to you that I was genuinely trying to be helpful or that I did seem to give a damn? Come on now, be honest and think about it.

Client: Well, yes (calms down a bit), but I'm also pretty damned pissed at you right now.

Therapist: Well, O.K. And maybe you have a good reason to be mad. But does that absolutely mean that I've *never* been at all helpful or caring towards you?

Client: No, it doesn't.

Client: I can't do anything right. Everything I touch turns to shit.

Therapist: Look … I know you are really upset about the blow-up with Kathy. It makes sense that it would upset you. At the same time, think for a minute—is it 100 percent accurate that you don't do *anything right*? What about last weekend when you guys did a great job resolving your differences of opinion. Yeah, this last episode was intense, *and* there clearly have been times recently when you've tackled a tough situation and made it work.

2. **Countering Overly Negative, Pessimistic Predictions:**

    Client: I'm never going to find someone who will love me.

    Therapist: You feel very discouraged now and that's the truth. But tell me, Doug, where is the evidence . . . where is the proof that you absolutely never will meet someone you can have a relationship with?

    Client: Well, there is no "proof," but that's how I feel.

    Therapist: And rightly so. It's been very discouraging for you to break up with Sally. But, especially now when you are feeling so upset, it doesn't make a lot of sense for you to make extremely negative predictions for the future. For one reason, doing so just increases your pain . . . it doesn't help. . . . And secondly, you *don't* have proof. There can be a big difference between *feeling* discouraged and, on the other hand, being absolutely convinced that the future is bleak.

3. **Gaining Perspective:** As discussed earlier, a borderline patient's intense emotional states often lead to feeling swallowed up in the moment, and losing perspective.

    Client: I am so furious, I can't stand it. How the hell could he have said that?! The son of a bitch! I won't ever be able to show my face around work again.

    Therapist: Obviously his comments really made you feel angry, and, I guess, pretty hurt, too. Right?

    Client: Yes.

    Therapist: I want to ask you something. Clearly this is upsetting now. Think about it. In all likelihood, how do you think you will feel about this twenty-four hours from now?

    Client: Well, still pretty upset.

    Therapist: O.K. How about forty-eight hours from now or this time next week?

    Client: Well, not nearly as upset, but I still don't know if I can ever forgive him.

    Therapist: Maybe not. It was very hurtful *and* it also sounds like when some time passes—even just a day or two—it probably won't seem quite as overwhelming.

    Client: True. (She is calmer.)

4. **Reframing:** This approach attempts to offer a new perspective for understanding one's feelings, needs, or reactions. The goal is twofold: First, to help move the person to a perspective of greater self-acceptance and self-compassion and second, to reduce affective intensity by countering the tendency to think or say:

"It shouldn't be that way!" or "I shouldn't feel this way!"

Client: I am so completely overwhelmed with sadness, I can't stand it. What the hell is wrong with me? I'm so screwed up.

Therapist: Barbara, I want to ask you something. You and I both know that you went through a lot of hell when you were a kid. You got hurt a *lot* and you were neglected a *lot*. Especially given your early life experiences, is it understandable to you that you'd be sensitive to these kinds of reactions and hurt now?

Client: Sure, I guess. But it seems like it hurts too much.

Therapist: It does hurt a lot. And what I am asking you is this—does this emotional pain make sense to you?

Client: Of course it does. (She looks sad, but less distraught.)

This last example warrants a few additional comments. This type of intervention, in my experience, often makes a dramatic difference in moments of intensely painful emotions. I think it does several things at once. Asking if an experience is understandable shifts it outside of the realm of good-bad, right-wrong. The shift of perspective allows our clients to step back a bit from the center of the emotional storm and become at least slightly more objective. Additionally, it encourages them to view the situation with greater self-compassion. Finally, it is a way for the therapist (albeit indirectly) to communicate "It's understandable to me." (Although for this to be helpful, that reply must come from the client.)

GENERAL STRATEGIES

An important objective in the treatment of BPD is to help our clients achieve a greater level of emotional and behavioral stability, and then to aid them in developing more effective coping skills. The weaker the ego functioning is, the more important it is to use stabilizing interventions, and avoid approaches that are evocative. However, it is important to note that it is almost never a case of all-or-none. Most times, therapists use a blend of these two major approaches, as the need is dictated in the moment. An exclusive reliance on supportive interventions may not be always appropriate. This was demonstrated in the Menninger Treatments Outcome Study that carefully evaluated the nuances of therapists' interventions in the psychotherapy of BPD (Gabbard 1996).

These researchers found that although a more supportive approach (i.e., stabilizing interventions) was usually indicated, not infrequently, some insight-oriented techniques were appropriately used. When done skillfully, both of these approaches can be very helpful for many borderline clients. These people do, of course, have legitimate needs to explore, express, and share deeply painful feelings, disturbing dreams, and traumatic memories. The trick is to use expressive interventions cautiously and to monitor the patient's response (both within the session and by assessing behavior between sessions).

When there is evidence of too much emotional dyscontrol or accelerated acting out, it is wise to carefully assess what you are doing in the sessions and then shift interventions in a more stabilizing direction. It may be tempting to explore some especially emotional or juicy material more deeply when it surfaces during a session. *But resisting the impulse to probe may be necessary when your goal is to promote more containment and control.*

As the therapist tracks moment-to-moment behavior (speech, emotional expression, body language, etc.), illustrated in Figure 4.1 as progressing from left to right, particularly noteworthy behaviors will emerge. These can be crucial moments when the therapist must judge whether or not to intervene. Such choice points occur hundreds of times in each session. Often, the therapist chooses not to intervene, but at certain times, a strategic comment or other type of intervention can make a difference. This, of course, is not a random decision, but one guided by the therapist's assessment: "What would be helpful in *this* moment?"

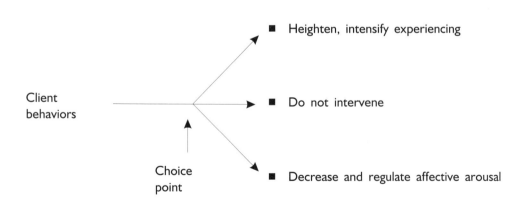

**Figure 4.1. Tracking Moment-to-Moment Material:
Choice Points and Intervention Decisions**

CHAPTER 5

Common Features in Various Treatments

Although many authors recommend somewhat different theories and models for the treatment of borderline personality disorders, it also is clear that there are certain elements of treatment that have been generally agreed upon. In their very insightful book, Waldinger and Gunderson (1987) describe eight common features that are summarized in this chapter. All are central aspects of successful treatment of BPD.

STABILITY OF THE THERAPEUTIC FRAME

Stability of the therapeutic frame refers to all activities that operate to define and maintain the conditions and limits of therapy, such as the times for meetings, beginning and ending sessions on time, limits on between-session phone calls, payment of fees, and maintenance of a strictly professional relationship between patient and therapist. All major theorists agree that these elements provide the important structure and stability so crucial for the successful treatment of borderline disorders.

INCREASED ACTIVITY OF THE THERAPIST

Prolonged silences and inactivity on the part of the therapist can evoke significant anxiety in BPD clients. Thus, most authors advise a more active, engaging kind of interaction for the therapist. In part, a more interactive therapist increases his/her sense of presence in the session, and can more successfully keep the client engaged (especially more engaged in the reality of the moment). This serves as a sort of anchor in the "here-and-now," and decreases the likelihood of the client regressing or becoming engulfed in overwhelming inner experiences.

TOLERANCE FOR NEGATIVE TRANSFERENCE REACTIONS

Here is where you earn your money as a therapist. As stated earlier, intense negative transferences are common with the treatment of BPD. They take place in therapy and in many, if not most, other relations outside of treatment. One major problem is that explosions of rage and devaluation are, as a rule, not met with compassion or neutrality (at least not outside of the therapeutic environment). Most people get very upset if they are viciously attacked, falsely accused, or lambasted in vile language. In the life experiences of borderline people, the predominant experience is: "I get upset" (the negative transference), then "Others either counterattack or massively withdraw." The repeated experience of this kind of interaction etches itself into already powerful schemas, e.g., "People hate me," "People reject me," or, "People are just no damned good."

Therapists are not there to be abused or to masochistically submit to hateful attacks. However, we must be prepared to act as shock absorbers, to contain these frontal assaults, and not to react (with counterattack or withdrawal). Therapists must reflect and understand, rather than react. Riding out such affective storms often proves to be a critical aspect of successful treatment.

MAKING CONNECTIONS

For borderline patients, impulsive emoting and action are the primary defenses against the awareness of inner painful feelings. Obviously, unreflected, impulsive behavior can have disastrous consequences. Most authors agree that *awareness* is essential for self-control. It may be helpful to consider that much of borderline behavior essentially is a stimulus-response. Awareness and some amount of cognitive activity (e.g., reflection) potentially can insert a wedge between the stimulus and response. Basically, making connections means helping clients to increase awareness, put feelings into words, and heighten their understanding that certain situations provoke strong emotions.

When borderline people are asked, "Why did you react that way?" following major emotional outbursts, many will quite honestly respond, "I don't know." This is the essence of stimulus-response. The stimulus sets off the response without any cognitive activity occurring in between. Here, the therapist may say, "Let's see what led up to this. Maybe we can figure out what happened that triggered this strong reaction." This begins the process of assessment and understanding that leads the client to make the connections; to "figure it out." To the extent that he/she can begin to do this, to think about it, to articulate it, and to make the connections between events, emotions, and actions, we have initiated a process that can help them achieve better self-control (Gabbard 1996a).

MAKING SELF-DESTRUCTIVE BEHAVIORS UNGRATIFYING

It is remarkable how unaware many BPD patients are that their behavior is maladaptive and self-destructive. This is the case because *in the moment* most severe acting out is experienced as necessary and helpful. (That is, the acting out is almost always accompanied by a sense of relief. Bear in mind that despite the ultimately negative consequences, these defenses *do* work to help the person avoid feeling potentially even more painful and engulfing emotions.) Furthermore, in the aftermath, the borderline person often engages in significant denial (ignoring or minimizing the severity of the negative consequences or externalizing the blame, e.g., "It was all her fault," or "He forced me to do it").

Most authors acknowledge the importance of addressing this problem. Usually this is accomplished by tactfully confronting patients with the reality of what they have done, and how it has hurt them. The therapist does the reality testing for the client. Here is a case example of the technique.

Case Example:

Therapist: "Mike, I know when you get to feeling extremely depressed, you drink a *lot* of alcohol and I think it numbs you at the time . . . and then for a while you don't feel as desperate. At the same time, it seems clear that those times when you get really drunk, you end up hurting yourself a lot. For instance, you've told me many times that you've been unable to go to work the next day . . . and how your job is on the line if you keep not showing up, or coming in late."

Client: "Yeah, but I can handle it, it's not that big a deal."

Therapist: "We may not see eye-to-eye on this, but I think it *is* a big deal. I suspect it would be very hard on you if you lost your job. I'd hate to see that happen and I do think the alcohol abuse contributes a lot to this."

Note: I have often felt inhibited about making comments like the one above, especially to clients who are very intelligent. Probably because it amounts to stating the obvious. However, it is important to underscore the fact that even very intelligent borderline patients are often oblivious to the consequences of their actions and in marked denial. We try to do for them what they cannot do for themselves—at least in the moment—and that is to see clearly the reality of their self-destructive behavior, to help them to reality test. The key to doing this successfully is to present the comment in a noncritical and compassionate way. The client needs to sense that you genuinely care about him/her.

DECREASING DANGEROUS ACTING OUT

Of course everyone has a right to want to avoid intensely painful emotions. However, as we have described, most borderline people go to great extremes to accomplish this avoidance, often by engaging in highly dangerous behaviors. Some acting out leads to progressively more severe drug addiction, some to significant physical mutilation, and some to contracting AIDS, or to death by suicide. A crucial goal in treating borderline clients is to put limits on acting out and to help clients to develop healthier strategies for reducing emotional pain.

In a study of negative therapeutic outcomes by Coleson, et. al. (1985), ten of the eleven cases studied revealed that failure to set limits was a key factor in the poor outcome. The therapists were judged to have commented on and interpreted maladaptive behavior, but they did no active limit setting.

FOCUSING ON THE "HERE AND NOW"

For anyone who had a history of emotionally traumatic events, it is natural and tempting to reflect on the past. However, to do so at any length with borderline clients can be risky. Often it opens them up to intensely painful feelings that can be overwhelming and destabilizing. Also, when the treatment plan is for brief therapy, it is unlikely that such old wounds can be adequately addressed. The preferred choice is to focus on problems in the client's present life situation. The goal is to promote more effective problem solving in the here and now and therapists must take charge of keeping the focus on *current* issues and problems.

MONITORING COUNTERTRANSFERENCE

As we know, borderline patients evoke all kinds of strong emotional responses in therapists—both common human responses and more uniquely personal reactions. The goal is not to avoid these reactions (because almost invariably they will occur). Rather, the objective is to stay alert to the emergence of countertransference reactions, recognize them for what they are, reflect, and as much as possible, avoid acting them out. One common mistake made by the novice therapist is to assume that the *good therapist* will not have countertransference reactions. Seasoned therapists know this is not a realistic expectation. All therapists, from time to time, are provoked into experiencing an array of feelings during treatment. What matters is how you deal with the feelings and how you understand them in the context of the particular client-therapist interaction.

Now, we are ready to begin to focus specifically on intervention strategies.

PART IV

TREATMENT STRATEGIES

CHAPTER 6

Prognosis and Treatment Goals

The parameters for psychotherapy addressed in this book are weekly sessions extending from four to eighteen months. In the following chapters very specific treatment strategies will be presented. It is important to first determine which borderline clients have the best chance of benefiting from this type of psychological treatment.

POSITIVE PROGNOSIS CRITERIA (INCLUSION CRITERIA)

Beyond the characteristics outlined in Chapter 1, in the section "Diagnostic Issues: Other Characteristics Related to Diagnosis, Prognosis, and Treatment Plans" (degree of intelligence, psychological mindedness, courage to face pain, etc.), three additional criteria make for a better prognosis, especially when considering brief treatment:

1. Some evidence of a positive interaction with the therapist

2. The existence of at least some social support and a desire to be with others

3. The existence of a fairly discrete, focal problem, i.e., a recently occurring stressor that has resulted in emotional upset or destabilization

---

EXCLUSION CRITERIA

The following characteristics suggest a poorer prognosis; that is, borderline people with these problems either may not benefit from brief therapy, or in a worst-case scenario, may actually become worse with only a course of brief therapy.

- Very severe dyscontrol manifested as significant violence towards others and/or a marked tendency for self-mutilation

- Profound cognitive disorganization or blatant psychotic symptoms

- Co-morbidity: BPD and bipolar disorder

- Pronounced schizoid traits (e.g., interpersonal aloofness)

- No interpersonal relationships outside the family of origin

- An inability or unwillingness to accept initial therapy contract and limit setting

- A history of *extreme* regression/decompensation in response to separation stresses. (Such people may become overly bonded to the therapist, and termination can be experienced as traumatic.) In such instances, a one-time crisis intervention session or even no therapy at all may be better solutions than involvement in brief therapy.

I believe that much can be done to help borderline clients in brief therapy. But the fact remains, a number of these folks need longer-term treatment or serial brief therapies and anything less is just not enough to help much.

GOALS OF SHORTER-TERM THERAPY

Let's get realistic. We must set aside notions of "cure" and yet not underrate the tremendous help we can offer to our borderline patients. The following is a set of reasonable goals that bear keeping in mind:

- To decrease dangerous acting out

- To eliminate substance abuse

- To achieve better containment and control of emotions and impulses

- To help prevent suicide and/or violence towards others

- To improve daily life coping skills (e.g., better problem solving and more adaptive interpersonal interactions)

- To resolve a focal problem (e.g., learning to better set limits in a troubled relationship; resolve a conflict at work; deal with the death of a parent)

I have provided consultation services to a number of therapists who came to me out of a sense of frustration and a feeling that they were failing in their treatment of borderline clients. Often, as they talked about their clients' histories and treatments, the following picture emerged. All the markers the therapists used to evaluate progress were negative. Their patients continued to be plagued by feelings of dysphoria and emptiness, they still had marked problems developing healthy relationships, and they continued to have only a marginal sense of self. Their therapists were all wondering "What am I doing wrong?"

On the one hand, it was undeniable that their clients were still dysfunctional and certainly not emotionally healthy. On the other hand, on closer inspection, it was discovered that a lot *had* changed in their clients' lives during the course of treatment. Many times there was abstinence from alcohol abuse, less chaos, less dangerous behavior, no self-mutilation, no suicide attempts, no psychosis. Maybe one client kept a job for the entire year or stayed out of jail. Perhaps another client formed an emotional attachment that seemed a little less dependent than previous attachments. Another avoided the frequent impulse to physically abuse her children. All-in-all, there was less suffering.

These were real and important gains. Although the therapists were feeling a sense of failure, in fact, the treatment did help considerably. If your aspirations are to make silk purses, don't pursue this line of work; but if you want to help reduce suffering in very wounded people, maybe this is the place to be. It may be humbling to have to downsize your expectations, but be clear—this is important work. In the treatment of borderline clients, the reduction of suffering is a legitimate goal.

CHAPTER 7

Therapeutic Strategies

THE CORNERSTONES OF SUCCESSFUL TREATMENT

To highlight some material discussed previously, I want to briefly list the five most important elements in treating borderline disorders. If therapists do nothing more than to provide these five critical elements, many BPD clients will benefit from therapy.

1. Maintain the frame

2. Ride out affective storms

3. Contain your countertransference

4. Maintain an atmosphere of utmost respect for the client

5. Provide a realistic and hopeful perspective

I want to add some brief comments to this last point. Many borderline patients are dominated by magical thinking, some with feelings of entitlement, and most with an intense need to reduce suffering. Therefore, many want, expect, or demand unrealistic outcomes from therapy. And when we can't magically produce these results, they may become deeply disappointed and/or enraged. For many of these people, early life relationships were characterized by not only neglect and abuse, but also by extreme invalidations and dishonesty. It is important for therapists not to repeat such interaction patterns. This is accomplished, in part, by openly discussing what we think are realistic treatment goals, and being honest about what we can and cannot provide. It is also important to state clearly what we are unwilling to provide, such as unlimited availability. Initially, such statements may be greeted with disappointment or anger, but ultimately this honest, straightforward approach will contribute to the client's perception of us as solid and reliable people.

Maintaining a hopeful perspective is not just wishful thinking. Longitudinal studies of BPD provide a measure of optimism for these people (McGlashan 1986; Stone et al. 1987 and 1988). For a majority of borderline patients, their twenties and thirties are years of chaos and great suffering. Yet some 65 to 75 percent of these people experience a noticeable change in their forties. For reasons that are not well understood, in their fourth decade, many borderline people start to settle down. What is seen is a diminution in emotional lability and impulsivity. This is accompanied by less erratic behavior and often by less troubled interpersonal relationships. Life begins to proceed on a more even keel. Some speculate that this may be due to neurobiological changes occurring with age, but, so far, this is just a hypothesis. Additionally, many of those who were initially diagnosed as BPD but later failed to meet criteria for this diagnosis had left an abusive relationship or had moved away from an emotionally toxic work environment (Gunderson 2003). Although borderline clients have a strong tendency to jump from one dysfunctional relationship to another, there are times when they experience a period of relative emotional quiescence. During such times they are in a better position to think clearly and to control impulsivity to the degree that they do not simply jump back into disturbed relationships. Sometimes they form intimate relationships with people who are more benign and do not get pulled into emotionally chaotic interchanges. In these cases, it seems apparent that longer-term, stable, and healthy relationships can help enormously in their growth and recovery.

So, if we can somehow help borderline clients through their more tumultuous years, and tide them over, there is real hope for a better, less chaotic life down the road. Helping to prevent suicide and self-mutilation, to avoid jail, and not burn too many bridges (interpersonally and occupationally) are extremely worthwhile goals in the treatment of BPD.

Note: It is also important to know that about 25 percent of borderline patients do *not* show this kind of improvement in midlife. In this poorer prognosis group the single most distinguishing feature is ongoing substance abuse. This fact underscores how important it is to push all of our BPD clients to seek treatment for chemical dependency problems. For many, doing that might be the single most important therapeutic goal of all.

ADVANTAGES OF TIME LIMITS

Most clinicians writing about shorter-term therapy have stressed the importance of establishing clear limits on the length of treatment (usually discussed with the patient during the first session). A cogent argument has been made that if the length of treatment is spelled out from the onset of the therapy, the knowledge of limited sessions facilitates positive outcomes in at least two ways. First, it provides a frame for the therapy. The client is not faced with a vaguely defined plan of treatment, but rather is explicitly told what to expect (i.e., how often they will be seen and how long therapy will last). This may be an especially important element in providing the structure that is so helpful in the treatment of borderline disorders. Knowing in advance how many times you plan to meet may also help to prevent regression, which more commonly occurs in long-term or open-ended therapies.

The second, often-cited, useful aspect of knowing how long therapy will be available is that when clients know the number of sessions is finite, that knowledge sometimes provides added impetus to "make something happen." Knowing that visits are limited, clients may be more likely to make every session count (e.g., they may be more inclined to get to the point or "down to business" regarding important issues).

Beyond this, a clearly defined limit to sessions may be especially helpful for borderline patients by reducing their tendency to become extremely attached to their therapists. Knowing that therapy is to be brief may help the client to anticipate the end of therapy, and reduce the likelihood of traumatic separation stress upon termination. This is especially important for therapists who are providing treatment for HMOs or managed-care companies and are limited in the number of sessions they can provide. To achieve this, therapists are urged not only to be exceptionally clear about the number of sessions that will be made available from the outset, but also to remind the client periodically—albeit tactfully—throughout therapy, how many sessions are left in the course of treatment. Being clear about the time constraints and keeping that information at a conscious level is an important way of taking care of the client. This clarity helps to avoid or minimize what otherwise might be an emotionally difficult time when the therapy comes to an end. Being clear about this demonstrates an understanding and acceptance of the client's vulnerability to losses.

One way to use the limited number of sessions is to have this as a way of framing treatment goals. Let's take a look at one example.

Framing Treatment Goals in Limited-Time Treatment

Therapeutic goals were discussed in Chapter 6. The limited number of sessions in shorter-term therapy can be used as a way of framing those treatment goals. Let's take a look at a case example:

Case Example: "Ms. Smith, we've met one time now, so let's talk about where we go from here. I want you to know that I can offer you a course of brief therapy. In our clinic this means that we can have up to ____ sessions together. Based on what we've talked about today, it seems to me that you have had some ongoing problems in relationships—and that you are feeling especially sensitive to rejections. I want to tell you that I think it's unlikely that in brief therapy we can completely resolve this problem. But I *do* believe that it's realistic for us to focus on helping you to do two things. First, to decide what you want to do regarding your current relationship, and second, to help you get back on your feet emotionally—so your life can seem less overwhelming and less chaotic to you. Do those seem like reasonable goals to you? If so, I'd be happy to work with you."

In a sense, the time limits give the treatment definition by providing a starting point, an ending point, and a time frame in which to spell out limited but realistic treatment goals. Also, this direct, straightforward approach may be healing in and of itself. So many borderline clients are accustomed to interpersonal interactions that are fraught with half-truths, vague messages, or out and out lies (especially in their families of origin). A no-nonsense approach to establishing the frame of therapy during the first session can set the stage for what is to come. It is a way of saying to the patient, "I am willing to work with you to provide what I can, to not make promises I can't keep, and to treat you with respect and decency by always being clear and honest." This same direct, honest style, is, of course, as important in all other interactions and it may turn out to be the crucial foundation on which a solid alliance is built.

EXPECTATIONS AND THERAPEUTIC CONTRACTS

This is an area that has been addressed by many authors, most notably Kernberg (1975) and Linehan (1993). The intent is to make it abundantly clear from the start of therapy, that there are certain expectations (both for the client and the therapist) and certain rules that *must* be followed for treatment to succeed. This is a very important part of creating the "frame," which is necessary to provide the structure that will help to contain affective storms and acting out.

In addition to providing structure, per se, therapeutic contracts are designed to address two common problems seen in the treatment of borderlines: reducing therapy-disruptive behaviors (e.g., dropping out prematurely or leaving during sessions) and behaviors that are potentially dangerous (to self and to others).

Many patients, and some therapists, experience the process of establishing rules and contracts as being too rigid. And, in a real sense, there is rigidity involved, but it is a type of rigidity born of firmness and the intent to do what is most likely to help the client. The way this is presented to the patient matters a lot. Let me offer an example of how this might be presented.

> **Case Example:** "Mr. Jones, we have spent some time together today and I think I have a pretty good idea about the problems you have been experiencing. I think psychotherapy can help you, but I want to be very frank with you about the *kind* of treatment that I am recommending and am willing to provide."

Then, some specifics are given. After the rules are outlined, the therapist should ask for the client's reaction, and, in particular, determine whether or not the client is willing to agree to the particular contract. Let's imagine that the client in our example is not sold on the idea, or is even upset with what is perceived to be either a too rigid or too cold approach. The therapist might reply:

> **Case Example**: "I know this sounds pretty rigid. There are certainly people who would not agree to these kinds of rules, and I can appreciate that.

Nevertheless, it is an approach to therapy that has been shown to be very helpful for people experiencing the kinds of difficulties you have. I think this kind of approach has a good chance of being helpful and it's the only kind of therapy I am able or willing to offer you. If for any reason, it just does not meet your needs or you don't want to participate, that's absolutely fine with me. It's your call. And, I'll be glad to refer you to some other therapists who may be willing to help you.

I do want you to carefully consider your decision and if you want to see me for this kind of treatment, I'd be glad to work with you."

The important points made in these examples are as follows:

1. The therapist is not negotiating any changes in the contract. It's a take-it or leave-it proposition. This is being firm.

2. It communicates the message that "I have an approach that I believe will be helpful," thus conveying confidence that this kind of treatment is likely to succeed.

3. It provides specific limits and guidelines that provide necessary structure.

4. It clearly acknowledges and honors the feelings, opinions, and decisions of the client. Ultimately, the client can take it or leave it, without shame or without feeling badgered by the therapist. This attitude of respect for the client's own personal opinions, feelings, etc. is a crucial theme that must run throughout all aspects of psychotherapy. It is a major way the therapist helps to promote the growth of the client's self.

SPECIFIC EXPECTATIONS, RULES, AND THE CONTRACT

Marsha Linehan (1993) has done an exceptionally good job of outlining specific features of the therapy contract, and readers are referred to her book for more details. What follows is derived from the work of both Linehan and Kernberg.

The Basic Contract

A. The Therapist's Responsibilities

  1. To be available for scheduled sessions

  2. To start on time and stop on time

  3. To do his/her best to understand the client and to provide helpful questions, comments, and feedback

4.   To maintain confidentiality

5.   To facilitate a process whereby the client can better take care of himself/ herself (i.e., to promote increasing autonomy in the client)

B.   The Patient's Responsibilities

I.   Attend sessions and not miss any, except in cases of emergencies or illness

2.   Stay for the entire session. Often during therapy sessions, clients may become very upset and may bolt, leaving sessions before the scheduled time is up. In establishing this rule, you can convey to clients that it is ultimately important for them to find ways to face difficult feelings without running away. Patients must understand that you will expect them to stay in the session and work through or try to understand whatever comes up, and you have confidence in them, that they will be able to do this. Once again, this communication of faith in their ability to deal with difficult issues helps to promote the self. It cannot be overemphasized that they need to deal with difficult material *during* sessions. Even though they may feel the urge to contact the therapist between sessions, this should not be done, except in cases of bona fide emergencies. You can say something along these lines: "A part of this kind of treatment that may feel difficult, but is so important, is for us to talk about important issues during sessions—not in between. It may be hard to do, but I'll be counting on you to do your best to follow this rule."

3.   Clients are expected to pay (the agreed-upon fee) for therapy at the end of each session. This is very important, because frequently power struggles or other types of client-therapist difficulties arise around the issue of fees. This needs to be dealt with in a straightforward, candid, business-like manner.

4.   There is an expectation that clients will actively participate in therapy, e.g., by speaking up freely about problem issues, being honest, doing homework, etc.

5.   Strictly following specific limits (rules). How much you make this a part of treatment depends on the client's level of functioning. *Very* firm limits are essential for low-level cases, especially those prone to severe regression, suicide, self-mutilation, and dangerous acting out. High-level borderline clients will also need limits, but may not need a formal "contract."

C.   Additional Limits Should Include the Following:

1.   If a client becomes highly suicidal between therapy sessions it is his/her responsibility to get to a psychiatric hospital or an emergency room to be evaluated. Clients are *not* to call the outpatient therapist. The client is certainly not expected to completely ward off self-destructive urges. Often this is not possible for them to do. But the expectation is that they must act to take appropriate measures to be seen in an Emergency Room, or at a hospital. The limit includes two factors believed to be important in this kind of treatment: The first is to maintain the frame, so that all (or nearly all) therapy occurs in the context of the scheduled therapy hour. Second, a strong message is conveyed along the lines of "although you may not be able to ward off suicidal feelings, I believe in you and I am confident that you will find it in yourself to act as a responsible adult, and take appropriate action." Again, this message is one of confidence and helps shore up the client's sense of self.

2.   If the client is hospitalized, any treatment given in the inpatient unit is provided by a hospital staff psychiatrist/therapist; i.e., the outpatient therapist does not treat the client during hospitalizations (although he/she does consult with the inpatient staff and is involved in treatment follow-up upon discharge).

3.   Setting the rules regarding between-session phone calls. This is always contingent on the therapist's own feelings about such calls. Generally, it is more advantageous to strongly discourage calls so that all of the issues are dealt with in sessions. Obviously, there needs to be some room for flexibility and exceptions. If the issue of limiting calls is not dealt with early in therapy, the stage is set for significant problems. Some clients will abuse this, and make more and more calls. As therapists, we have a legitimate need to have lives away from work. The overly solicitous therapist who does not deal with this issue early on may find himself/herself, at some point, overwhelmed with phone calls. The results can be increasing resentment in the therapist (an emotion often sensed by our clients), or, at some point, a direct confrontation with the client about the excessive calls. Often, the response to this is hurt feelings. Frequent phone calls can also promote maladaptive regression. It is always advisable to set limits ahead of time before things get out of hand.

Limit setting generally should be directed towards three issues: behavior that threatens the safety of the client, the safety of others, and the therapeutic process itself. Beyond this, limit setting also plays an important role in maintaining a positive therapeutic alliance.

Jeffrey Young (1996) has said that many therapists operate from their own "self-sacrifice" schema, which makes it very tempting to bend over backwards for clients. This may be especially true when we encounter these profoundly wounded people. One way this manifests is in a loosening of limits.

It is a common experience for therapists to fail to set limits firmly enough; this often appears as accepting an ever-increasing number of between-session or late-night telephone calls. The therapist may feel a pull to "rescue" borderline clients who seem to be in an almost constant state of crisis or emotional urgency. The therapist over-extends, and ultimately begins to feel worn out and resentful. A good rule of thumb is to ask yourself early on, "If this behavior continues or escalates, am I likely to resent it?" If the answer is "yes," then it's best to set limits and to set them as soon as possible.

If therapists have already gone beyond a certain limit and are currently feeling resentment, the following example may serve as a model to approach the issue with the patient.

> **Case Example:** "Jerry, I want to talk to you about something. During the past few weeks you have been very distressed and have called me a number of times between sessions . . . sometimes late at night. You very well may want and need a lot of support, especially lately. It's important for me to be honest with you about this. If there is a very severe crisis (you may want to say, if it is a truly life-or-death crisis) I *do* want you to call. But if it's not extremely serious, I would like to ask you to do your best to talk with me during sessions" (or, "please limit it to no more than one call per week," depending on the therapist's preference).
>
> "I want to be very clear with you about why I'm requesting this. For me to function well in my work, it is essential that I get rest and time away from work. I want to do a good job with my clients, and I know that getting adequate rest is essential. Also, I want to clearly acknowledge that I know you may genuinely want or need more contact or support. If you think that our once-a-week sessions simply are not enough, maybe we need to look into finding you a support group to supplement what you are getting from therapy."

This kind of direct, honest presentation provides empathy while avoiding judgments about the legitimacy of the client's neediness. It sets a limit and also models self-protective, self-nurturing behavior (as the therapist shares his/her own needs and limits). It may be necessary to add some version of the following, with some clients:

> "I know that if I get too many after-hours calls, I might reach a point where I'll resent it. I want to be able to help you, and I know I would not be as helpful to you if I felt any kind of inward resentment."

Very often our BPD clients worry about others becoming angry, resentful, or rejecting towards them. They are especially concerned that their own neediness will alienate others, including the therapist. Thus, directly addressing this concern not only helps to establish a limit, per se, it also communicates to the client what is truly OK and what is not with regard to between-session contacts.

Finally, the last thing our clients need is to sense that we are irritated or disgusted with them. Borderline clients are often very sensitive people who will sense our true inner feelings, even if we try to hide them. Direct, honest limit setting is one of the very best hedges against the countertransference difficulties that are so commonly encountered in the treatment of BPD.

Consequences of Breaking the Contract

These are the basic elements of a contract. They can be spelled out and agreed upon verbally; they can also be put in writing, with the therapist and the client both signing the agreement. This is especially helpful in the treatment of very severe border-line clients. After the therapist describes the limits, he/she must tell the client what will happen if the rules are broken. The most stringent consequence is, "If you are unable or unwilling to follow these guidelines, then I will not treat you."

There are times when I think it is helpful to soften this a bit, e.g., "It is not my intention to seem unduly harsh about this, but I am convinced, as are many other therapists, that these fairly rigid guidelines ultimately prove very important to a good outcome in psychotherapy. I do want to work with you and I expect that you'll be able to follow through with this agreement. But, once again, let me emphasize, if these rules are not OK with you, I can certainly understand, and I will be glad to refer you to another therapist who may have a different approach." Then, the ball is in the client's court.

Of course, for this approach to work, it needs to be strictly followed. If necessary, the therapist *must* be prepared to follow through with consequences. In my own practice, the first time a rule is broken, I use it as an opportunity to re-address the contract and the consequences. I do not terminate therapy at that point, but emphasize that no matter what, I will the next time (a sort of two-strikes-and-you-are-out). Many clients either misunderstand the original contract, or more often do not really believe that the therapist will actually terminate treatment. Your job then, is to set them straight.

I must confess that this very directive, hard-nosed approach goes against my grain (especially because I was influenced a lot by the work of Carl Rogers). But the bottom line is this approach works. It is an especially powerful way to build structure into the treatment, and ultimately contributes a great deal to reducing chaos and instability.

REDUCING VULNERABILITY FACTORS

In addition to core psychological deficits, such as affective instability, other factors often erode the borderline person's already marginal control. These factors fall into two broad categories; one involves neurobiology and the other focuses on interpersonal interactions and lifestyle. These are concrete things that can and should be addressed in every treatment case. Let's take a closer look.

Neurobiologic Vulnerability

The comments made here apply to everyone, but are especially important to address in the treatment of BPD. Sleep is a very fragile biological function; in many people it is easily interrupted by even minor stresses. Significant sleep disturbances can have a profound effect on cognitive and emotional functions. During times of crisis, almost without exception, borderline people experience at least some degree of sleep impairment.

Sleep Disturbances

Studies of sleep in sleep laboratories have found that all people go through the various stages of sleep during each night. These stages range from light sleep to deep sleep, and are measured precisely with an electroencephalograph (EEG), which measures brain activity. Sleep is roughly divided into two types: (1) REM (rapid eye movement) sleep and (2) non-REM sleep. During REM sleep, the brain is highly active. This is the time during which most dreaming occurs. Non-REM sleep contains four stages ranging from 1 to 4, with stages 3 and 4 containing a particular type of brain wave activity referred to as slow-wave sleep (or deep sleep). Most stage 3 and stage 4 sleep is seen during the first half of the night. REM periods become longer as the night progresses. (See Figure 7.1.)

Experimental studies have shown dramatically that if the amount of deep sleep is reduced or eliminated, there are significant consequences for the individual. In particular, often after only two nights of sleep deprivation (selectively deprived of stages 3 and 4) volunteer subjects experience the following:

- Significant daytime fatigue

- Difficulties with thinking (e.g., poor concentration, impaired memory, etc.), and most notably

- Decreased emotional controls

Changes in emotional functioning include the following:

- Irritability

- Lowered frustration tolerance, and

- Decreased ability to control or inhibit the expression of emotions in general

Increased anxiety often has an impact on sleep. It can result in insomnia (especially initial insomnia difficulty falling asleep) and, in general, an erosion of deep sleep. Additionally, a number of substances can interfere with sleep; most commonly these include alcohol and caffeine.

Alcohol Use

Alcohol, if ingested in moderate to heavy amounts, causes sedation and may help people to fall asleep. Many people when under stress turn to alcohol to numb emotional pain and to fall asleep. Unfortunately, alcohol is a solution that backfires. A few hours after ingesting alcohol, some of the metabolic by-products of alcohol hit the brain and actually cause arousal. Many if not most people who abuse alcohol will report such middle-of-the-night awakenings. This is one very important reason for insisting that *all* alcohol-abusing BPD patients get treatment for substance abuse.

Caffeine Use

It is widely known that caffeine can interfere with sleep; it is especially notorious for causing initial insomnia. For this reason, many people avoid the use of caffeine in the afternoon or evening. However, what is not appreciated by most people is that caffeine use can also cause an increase in middle-of-the-night awakenings and a decrease in the total amount of *deep* sleep (DSM IV, APA 1994). It is important to emphasize that this can occur even in the absence of initial insomnia. So there are many of our clients who use a lot of caffeine, do not experience initial insomnia, and thus conclude that the caffeine does not affect their sleep (unaware that, although they may be sleeping, it is an inefficient kind of sleep; lacking the very important stages of deep sleep). If you talk to clients about reducing caffeine, many will pooh-pooh the idea, not appreciating how much their caffeine intake is actually causing sleep impairment and the resulting increase in emotional dyscontrol.

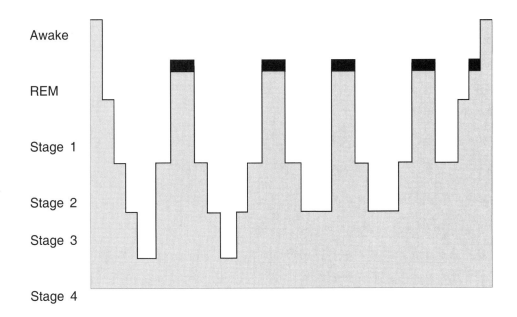

Figure 7.1. The Sleep-Wake Cycle in a Typical Adult During One Night

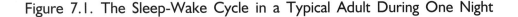

It is important to take a caffeine history on all patients. It takes two minutes to do and is a high-yield intervention. Here is how to do this. The general guidelines are that, if the person ingests more than 250 mg of caffeine per day (regardless of the time of day ingested) there is some likelihood of it affecting sleep. If they take 500 mg or more per day, it is *highly* likely to cause a sleep disturbance. A list of caffeine-containing products is provided in Table 7.1.

It is amazing how so many of our clients get into the habit of drinking a lot of caffeine, especially when they are under stress. Caffeine combats fatigue and provides some transient mood elevation. However, in the long run, it further compromises the borderline person's abilities for maintaining emotional stability. Encouraging clients to eliminate caffeine often makes a big difference (but anticipate some resistance from them when you suggest this, because most simply will not believe that it can really help). The key to reducing caffeine use is to have the client cut back gradually, e.g., over a period of three to four weeks. Abrupt discontinuation can result in caffeine withdrawal symptoms (e.g., jitterinesss, anxiety, insomnia, and headaches).

Table 7.1: Caffeine Content of Common Substances*

Beverages			Over-the-Counter Drugs	
Coffee	6 oz	125 mg	Appetite-control pills	100–200 mg
Decaf coffee	6 oz	5 mg	No Doz	100 mg
Tea	6 oz	50 mg	Vivarin	200 mg
Green tea	6 oz	30 mg	Anacin	32 mg
Hot cocoa	6 oz	15 mg	Excedrin	65 mg
Caffeinated soft drinks	12 oz	40–60 mg	Extra Strength Excedrin	100 mg
Prescription Drugs			Midol	132 mg
Cafergot	100 mg		Vanquish	33 mg
Fiorinal	40 mg		Triaminicin	30 mg
Darvan compound	32 mg		Dristan	16 mg

* Source: FDA National Center: Drugs and Biologics (as cited in Avis 1993).

Circadian Cycles

The stabilization of the circadian (twenty-four-hour cycle) rhythm can also aid in restoring normal sleep. Three activities have been shown to be quite helpful in bringing this about.

1. Establish regular bedtimes and times for awakening. This may not be agreeable to many clients, but it is often very successful if done correctly. The circadian rhythm organizes itself around highly regular patterns of exposure to light and dark, and this is best achieved by maintaining a regular sleeping schedule.

2. A second activity also helps stabilize the circadian rhythm: exposure to early morning bright light. This is best done for at least 20 minutes upon awakening and with exposure to very bright light (2500 lux or above); this can be accomplished by exposure to outside light or the use of a commercially available light box.

3. Finally, the third activity is regular exercise. A program of regular exercise (especially aerobic-level exercise) has many benefits (e.g., improved physical health, increases in brain serotonin levels, enhanced physical pain tolerance, etc.). Exercise also has been shown to increase the amount of time spent in deep sleep.

Simply suggesting to BPD clients that they reduce alcohol and caffeine, get bright light exposure, and exercise is often unsuccessful. They won't take the suggestions seriously or they will have difficulty following through. I have found it significantly more helpful to give them a brief lecture about sleep and sleep cycles, point out the need for deep sleep and how this has an impact on emotional functioning, and then introduce the issues involving caffeine, exercise, etc. It is often helpful to tell them that taking action to change these habits is a very direct way to regain at least some control over their brain functioning and, ultimately, their ability for increased self-control. Making such changes empowers them. These are direct, concrete actions that allow us to get more out of therapy.

Neurobiological destabilization also occurs in many Axis I psychiatric disorders (especially in major depression and bipolar disorder). Once again, sleep disturbances are likely to play a major role in some aspect of depressive symptomology (e.g., decreased emotional control). When there is evidence of co-morbid major depression or other Axis I disorders, psychotropic medication is indicated (see Chapter 10 for specifics on pharmacotherapy) both to treat the specific disorder, and to stabilize sleep.

Chaos Management Skills

Most borderline people are extremely disorganized, but for that matter, so are many of us higher functioning folks, too. As simple as it may seem, teaching BPD clients some basic chaos management skills is a helpful intervention. These are techniques many of us use naturally, and include the following:

1. Keeping a calendar/appointment schedule book. This helps them to remember important things and to anticipate upcoming events. Many borderline people feel so fragmented and disorganized that they forget appointments, or do things at the last minute, which simply increases their sense of being out of control.

	Must Do (Necessary)	**Will Do If I Have Time**
Highly Meaningful or Pleasurable	Spending time with my husband Getting enough sleep	Gardening Knitting
Not Meaningful or Pleasurable	Washing dishes Paying bills	Visiting with people I don't really like

Figure 7.2. Degree of Necessity

2. Making daily "to do" lists with two columns, one as "must do" and another as "will do if I have time," to help them practice prioritizing tasks. (This is also helpful for them to learn how to move away from extreme black-or-white thinking, which is such a critical part of their cognitive difficulties.)

3. Categorizing daily life activities and obligations. Suggest that they do this project for one week, to get a sense of the activities that occupy their lives. This is also a way to prioritize, but it goes a step beyond. This is an exercise (which can be done in therapy sessions or as "homework") that can help people become clearer about how they really feel and to define what life activities are really important to them. The 4 x 4 matrix shown in Figure 7.2 is a helpful way to do this. Let's look at an example.

In this example, washing dishes is not especially meaningful or enjoyable for the client, but ultimately it is a necessary life activity, while spending time with her husband is judged to be necessary for her well-being and personally meaningful. Gardening is not essential to her life, although she likes doing it. Finally, time that she spends with people she does not like (probably an obligation) is neither meaningful nor necessary. Activities in this particular quadrant are often things to consider eliminating from one's life.

I want to emphasize that above and beyond the use of this matrix in bringing some organization into one's life, another real value is that it helps clients identify and acknowledge what their own values, needs, priorities, and interests really are. This is a concrete exercise that can help the client towards more clarity about these issues, and, ultimately, it contributes to building a more solid and authentic self.

Setting Limits

Again, setting limits is a problem that many of us face. Many sources of stress arise from interpersonal relationships where one person feels used, abused, or taken advantage of by another. It is one thing to deal with distressing feelings internally; it is yet another to go directly to the source and negotiate changes in a relationship or to set firm limits with another. Many borderline people grew up in homes where their needs were seldom recognized, or worse yet, their expression of needs or feelings was met with harshness and punishment. A common outcome for this is that self-assertion was stifled and they sank into passivity and subjugation. Several examples will illustrate this.

- A woman seldom responds directly to her highly critical husband who frequently belittles and humiliates her in front of others. She grits her teeth and feels inwardly hurt and furious, and the abuse continues.

- A nurse is repeatedly asked to take on more and more duties at work. The unrealistic demands can be accomplished only by working through lunch hours or staying after hours, for which there is no extra pay. He does his work, complies, and feels increasingly exhausted and ill-used.

- A man longs for more contact with his wife. However, over the past year she has become progressively more consumed in her work. He feels lonely and desperate for greater intimacy, but is afraid to approach her about his need, for fear that she will explode at him.

- A young woman has mastered the courage to move away from home and away from a controlling and engulfing mother. Her mother calls her daily and complains about physical problems, and blames her daughter for "abandoning" her. The daughter feels obliged to visit her mother often and bitterly resents mom's manipulative phone calls.

In each instance, the person is encountering ongoing stresses and has not developed the skills to say "no" or to set limits. A part of this may be seen simply as a skills deficit (i.e., something that they have not yet, but could potentially learn). However, most of the time it's more than this. For many borderline clients, there are basic deficits in the self that play a role in this inability to set limits, including: not really knowing what he/she wants, likes, or doesn't like; not feeling that he/she has a right to speak out or take a stand; or feeling extremely vulnerable to the other person's potentially negative response (e.g., anger, guilt trips, etc.).

To the extent that we can give permission to and encourage our clients to set limits on others, we are not only helping them to reduce sources of ongoing distress, but these actions also may help solidify their inner sense of self.

Once again, being very directive or making specific suggestions and offering advice may rub therapists the wrong way. It may be helpful, however, to consider that on an emotional level, many of these people are like two-year olds. And, as we do with children, it may be necessary to give specific suggestions and to recommend particular coping strategies. This can be followed up with behavioral rehearsal (within the session) and feedback.

I was once told quite bluntly by one of my borderline clients who is a physician, "John, you are always so careful not to insult my intelligence by telling me what to do. But you need to know that the times you have given me specific advice have been extremely helpful. I need that kind of guidance. It helps a lot." He was right.

This necessitates walking a fine line between truly helpful guidance and what may be seen as infantilizing the client. Too much or inappropriate advice can feed into increasing dependency and regression. So it's a matter of clinical judgment. The starting point must be in first determining how the client really feels and what he/she defines as important. When this is accomplished, your specific suggestions are more likely to be helpful and in the service of your client's growth and autonomy.

Avoiding Toxic People

The impact of highly dysfunctional interactions with others is enormous and likely the most common factor that accounts for emotional destabilization. One technique that can be helpful is a *toxic-people list*. Suggest to the client to take a piece of paper and draw a line down the middle. Then encourage them to list everyone they know (friends, family, co-workers, etc.), placing those who frequently provoke trouble in the left-hand column—for example, people who are belittling, shaming, critical or judgmental, people who provoke arguments, who are unreliable or who contribute to the client's substance abuse, and people who constantly ask too much of the client. The right column is for more supportive and healthy relationships; e.g., people who accept, love, encourage, help, or understand the nature of the client's disorder.

This seemingly simple approach aids in critical thinking. As the client becomes more clear about which people routinely contribute to distress, then they can choose to actively avoid them, keep contacts brief, or, if possible, be coached in doing conflict resolution and relationship repair. Many people feel obligated to have contact with family members or certain friends, even when they pay a great cost emotionally. They have the right to identify such potential hot spots and practice avoidance. This is analogous to learning how to safely walk through a field of landmines. A part of the success of this approach hinges upon the client's ability to take in that they have a right to choose to avoid problematic relationships as a form of self-protection.

INCREASING SELF-NURTURING, POSITIVE EXPERIENCES, AND MASTERY

There are two forces at work in the lives of every person. One is the degree of negative emotions being experienced (frustration, loneliness, sadness, anger, etc.). The other is the positive side of the ledger: experiences that enliven, enrich, and vitalize.

So often psychotherapy and psychiatric treatment aims to reduce unpleasant symptoms, but neglects or underemphasizes the more positive side of living. One mark of emotional health is the capacity to engage in, acknowledge, and enjoy aspects of life even while in the midst of emotional crises. It is a major way we avoid collapse into utter despair.

Conversely, an important feature of more severe personality dysfunction is a deficit in one's capacity to embrace and experience the positive aspects of life. Aaron Beck (1976) and other cognitive therapists have addressed this issue in detail by focusing on the cognitive distortions commonly encountered in depression. Depressed individuals often lose the capacity to experience joy (i.e., anhedonia, which may be largely mediated neurochemically). In addition, cognitions and reality testing become impaired in a particular way, where attention is focused almost exclusively on negative events. This kind of selective attention not only accentuates the negative, it also involves an inattention to positive events. So, when something nice happens, for example, receiving a compliment, the depressed individual either fails even to notice it or interprets it in a negative way, e.g., "Well, they said I did a good job, but they were just trying to be nice. I know I did a lousy job." This kind of cognitive tunnel vision results in an overall view of the world that is especially bleak.

Borderline people also fall prey to this same process. A good deal of their experience of overwhelming pain and extreme vulnerability is accounted for by this maladaptive style of perceiving reality. How can we help them with this?

Daily Activity Diary

First, it must be acknowledged that many of the events in their lives are objectively unpleasant. The goal is not to get them to deny reality. Some of their painful issues must be faced. However, a helpful intervention is aimed at improving their ability to notice, acknowledge, and feel the results of positive events. This approach has long been used by behaviorists and involves keeping a daily activity list. A small spiral notebook can serve well. The patient is told that the goal is to get better at noticing positive events. Patients are requested to carry the notebook with them each day and to frequently jot notes in the book. The notes need to be kept brief. The patient also needs to grade each note with a symbol, after each entry: **P** (pleasure), **M** (mastery: accomplishing something), or **I** (an event that felt important or personally meaningful).

Let's consider an example from my client, Arthur:

- The weather is nice today. (P)

- I got to work on time. (M)

- Judy looked friendly and said hello to me. (P)

- I got a good deal buying some lawn furniture. (M)

- My sister called and we had a good talk. (P, I)

- I felt upset with my boss, but I didn't blow up. I handled it pretty well. (M)

How can this help? Often by the end of a day, our borderline clients reflect on their day and tend to conclude "It was a lousy day," "Everything I did, I screwed up," or "I'm completely overwhelmed." The activity diary helps to improve the accuracy of reality testing. Let's assume my client Arthur did have a rough day and also recorded some positive events as listed above. When he looks at the diary, it becomes easier to remember the positive experiences. His new conclusion may be "I had a tough day. There were a lot of unpleasant experiences, *and,* thank goodness, there were some positive things too." This is an important change in perspective. The newer, more accurate conclusion is less likely to leave Arthur feeling 100 percent bad about himself or about his day.

Another version is the use of a "gratitude diary." At the end of each day, our client is encouraged to write in the diary, at least two events that occurred for which he/she felt grateful.

Self-Nurturing

Another intervention is aimed toward helping our clients actually engage in more self-nurturing activities. Again, it has been well documented that in the lives of chronically depressed clients, positive life activities are few and far between. This is because in the throes of depression, people often withdraw and become progressively cut off from life-sustaining activities. So too with borderline clients.

On one level this intervention encourages the client to weave more positive experiences into daily life. On another level, and maybe the aspect that is even more important, it is a message to the client: "It's OK for you to be good to yourself." This is a message rarely heard from others during the borderline person's early life. It may be taken in only superficially, but, at times, it may become part of a new and healthier introject; a less harsh and more self-nurturing introject.

The Value of Homework

Another approach that can be helpful is to develop a positive activity list. The therapist and client work together to develop a list of activities that the patient has identified as potentially either enjoyable or meaningful. (Please see appendix B for a helpful list of positive activities.) Then the client is encouraged to plan out a schedule and engage in a certain number of activities between the current and the next session. This works best if the person makes specific plans for specific days, and if the therapist follows up during the next session, to check on the client's progress. It should be emphasized, however, that one of the most common reasons homework interventions often do not work, is that therapists fail to do follow-up (either they forget or they feel inhibited about inquiring). Needless to say, it is critical to pursue this in later sessions for it to be effective.

THE PRIMARY FOCUS: "HERE AND NOW"

For therapy to be successful, it is very important to agree upon a specific goal or problem during the first session, and to define this as the major focus of all subsequent therapy sessions. It will be the therapist's job to make sure the sessions stay on track (i.e., stick to the focus). Even though past hurtful experiences may be exceptionally important to some clients, in general, it is strongly advised that a particular focus be chosen that deals with *current* life circumstances. One way to frame this is to ask, "Why is life not working for you *now*?" Understanding this (the precipitating events, the reactions, and consequences), and then developing effective coping strategies is key to successful treatment. Thus, at those times when the client's attention shifts to other issues (e.g., past hurts, childhood experiences, etc.) it will become important for the therapist to take action and redirect the therapy, back to the agreed-upon focus. This can be tricky to do because we do not want to hurt clients or leave them feeling misunderstood. Let's look at an example.

> **Case Example:** It's session number three for Sharon. She had agreed on a primary focus with the therapist in her first session. The decision was for her to come to terms with the recent loss of a boyfriend. (He had left her for another woman.) In the current session she talks about her loss, and begins to liken it to when she was very young and felt rejected by her father.
>
> Here is the tricky part. We do need to know something about her prior experience to provide the context for understanding her current areas of emotional vulnerability. We also do not want to repeat the experience of rejecting her. If we refuse to listen to her feelings about early life events, she rightly may again feel a sense of rejection. So, the therapist might say, a few minutes into her discussion about her childhood:
>
> "Sharon, I want to interrupt you for a minute. You are starting to talk about some very unpleasant experiences you had when you were young. Obviously this is very painful material to bring up.... I do want to know about that time in your life, and we can go ahead and talk about it some, if you wish. But, as we agreed in our first session, it's going to be very important for us to stay focused on the more recent issue of this break-up with Stan. I don't intend to ignore the memories you are sharing with me now, but I do want to strongly encourage you to get back to more recent issues. I think that's where we have our best shot at resolving the problems you are facing at this time in your life."

I can imagine more psychodynamically oriented therapists cringing as they read the last paragraph. Let me be clear. I believe that the prior experiences (and how these are currently manifested by way of memories and enduring cognitive schemas) are tremendously important both in terms of how they have an impact on Sharon's life and on how we, as therapists, can use such data to help understand why she is currently so vulnerable. The issue is, however, will it be productive to really explore this material in detail with the client, especially early in treatment when the client is still fragile? Most of the time, it will not.

There are risks involved in the decision to explore the past. One risk is that it shifts the focus away from current problems. Another is that there is a real possibility that opening up old wounds may precipitate the eruption of intense emotions and regression. In briefer forms of treatment, we may not have time to adequately work through this material. It is in this kind of situation that therapy can be harmful. This may be compared to a patient undergoing surgery. Halfway through the procedure the doctor stops and says, "Time's up, we've gotta stop," yet the patient is lying on the operating table, cut open. Maybe this is an extreme analogy, but I think my point is clear.

Do No Harm

I have a lot of respect for the value of fostering deep awareness and of the process of working through old pain. If time allows, this is often extremely helpful. However, wanting to do no harm is more important than my own theoretical biases, and also I want to use interventions that have the highest likelihood of being helpful in the context of brief therapy. Keeping the therapy focus anchored in the "here and now" (i.e., current problems) is an important therapeutic activity.

Focus and Stabilization

Another aspect of the "here and now" perspective is that it can be used to help stabilize clients who are in the throes of intense emotion. At times of severe affective dyscontrol, borderline clients often become swept away by their strong emotions. They become overwhelmed and quickly lose perspective. One helpful approach to use during a session is to intervene actively and make suggestions designed to help the client feel more "grounded." These techniques encourage the patient to get in touch with concrete aspects of the present moment. Let's illustrate this with an example.

Case Example: Jack begins to feel overwhelmed with sadness and anxiety as he talks about a terribly upsetting encounter he recently had with his mother. The therapist comments:

Therapist: "Jack, please listen to me. You are feeling really overwhelmed right now. We can talk more later about the episode with your mother. Right now, however, I want to help you settle down so you can feel more in control of yourself. OK?

Jack: "OK, sure."

Therapist: "Jack, listen to me. It's 10:30 a.m., Tuesday morning, and you are here in the office with me. Look around the room for a minute, and be sure to take it all in. It's just you and me, here together. Your mother is not in this room. You had a tough time with her yesterday, but that was yesterday. We can talk more about that later. For now, just try to get anchored in the here and now . . . notice your feet, flat on the floor. Notice your back against the chair . . . pay attention to how you are breathing. Now, how are you doing?"

Jack: "Somewhat better."

This is called a "grounding technique." It strives to shift the focus of attention from "then and there" to "here and now," shifting awareness away from distressing cognitions and memories to current, less intense realities. It's not magic; it's simply an easy technique that will help your client regain perspective and reduce emotional arousal. Clients can also learn to use this technique with very good results outside of the therapy setting.

I will close this chapter with a metaphor that may help the client to endure moments of significant distress: Imagine that someone is at the seashore, wading in the water (see Figure 7.3). An unexpectedly large wave washes over the person. For a moment he/she is completely covered by water. In that instant it might be natural to think "I am going to drown." Yet if one maintains perspective and simply holds on, in a few seconds the wave will pass. The key is to appreciate that the deep water is transient. The deep waves of emotional turmoil are similarly transient, although in the midst of the feelings, it can certainly seem as though they will never end. The ability to avoid being swallowed up in the moment, and appreciating the transient nature of emotional waves is a very important aspect of tolerating distress.

Figure 7.3. Emotional Waves Are as Transient as Ocean Waves.

CHAPTER 8

Therapeutic Strategies for Reducing Emotional Arousal and Dyscontrol

It may be helpful to view the propensity for dyscontrol as containing the following five critical elements:

1. A neurobiologically based tendency for excessive emotional sensitivity (such that the person is inclined to experience emotions very intensely and/or to have a lower threshold for stimulation, such that strong emotions are evoked by even minor stressors).

2. Difficulty with behavioral inhibition, thus more likely to display feelings externally in the form of affect-driven actions and physiological manifestations of emotion (e.g., tearfulness, trembling, etc.). Note: some people may be exquisitely sensitive, yet able to contain emotional expression and thus not reveal emotions outwardly. Most borderline people have both sensitivity *and* excessive behavioral dysinhibition.

3. The tendency to commit cognitive errors that result from distorted perceptions and inaccurate conclusions. The result is that borderline people often perceive many situations of even minor stress, as catastrophic. The distorted thinking dovetails with the underlying sensitivity and excessive reactivity to heighten arousal and dyscontrol.

4. Another aspect of the propensity for dyscontrol is born of poor judgment. Borderline individuals often unwittingly seek out connections or interactions with other people who are also emotionally disturbed or provocative. The result is that interactions are likely to be quite problematic and stormy.

5. Finally, most borderline people have not developed adequate outlets for the expression of important and legitimate feelings.

FACILITATING MORE ADAPTIVE COGNITIVE OPERATIONS

The interventions discussed in this chapter aim to reduce arousal and to promote greater emotional control and address each of the five areas outlined above.

Stop and Think

When faced with emotion-provoking experiences, people have two primary ways of responding. The first is with reactive behavior. (In the extreme this involves impulsive actions and the outward display of emotions.) The second avenue of response is to inhibit action and engage in some sort of cognitive reflection (e.g., careful assessment of what has just happened, critical thinking regarding possible actions and their likely consequences).

As mentioned before, so much of a borderline person's life is dominated by impulsive reactions. When affect is very intense, people lose perspective and cannot engage in critical thinking, which is necessary for cognitive techniques to be effective. The first order of business, as noted above, is to spot potential landmines ahead of time and strategically avoid them (e.g., avoid contact with certain toxic people). However, if the client begins to experience a welling up of intense emotion, it is critical to take action as soon as possible to reduce affect arousal. The therapist, in reviewing recent emotional catastrophes with the client, can coach the client to engage in better self-monitoring in order to identify early warning signs of what may escalate into an emotional meltdown. At that moment, if at all possible, you instruct the client to take a *time-out* (i.e., remove oneself from close proximity with another, e.g., go into the back yard). Time-outs alone can work towards deescalation. Often, once an argument is started, both parties end up throwing more gas on the fire, and this is a key factor in elevating the encounter to one of crisis magnitude.

The next approach is to help the client engage in some activity that directly reduces emotional arousal. (Note that at this time the client may still be so emotionally upset that they cannot yet engage in any cognitive coping skills. Thus, you must help them develop self-calming techniques.) Two of the most effective actions are intense physical exercise (ten to fifteen minutes of jogging or brisk walking) or crying. It is important to help them learn how to cry without negative self-talk. Often crying spells are accompanied by ruthless attacks on the self, e.g., "What the hell is wrong with me?!!", "Here I go again . . . I'm just screwed up." Coach them into being able to know that crying is a very natural physical response to intense emotions and most people who give themselves permission to cry experience a noticeable decrease in sadness, anger, and fear, often within two to three minutes (Frey 1983).

When time-out and exercise or crying have worked to turn the volume down on affective arousal, most clients will then be capable of using cognitive coping strategies.

The goal in facilitating more adaptive cognitive functioning is threefold: First, better cognitive functioning is a major coping skill that is used to modulate affect arousal and our aim is to enhance this ability. Second, with more careful appraisal and thoughtfulness, the resulting actions taken by the client are less likely to be maladaptive. Third, in these moments when emotional reaction is inhibited, when thinking takes place, and decisions are made, individuals are more apt to experience their resulting actions as being a *choice*. This third point is important to emphasize. When we consider the phenomenology of the borderline person's life experiences, many times, if not most of the time, he/she feels swept up or carried away by intensely strong feelings. There is seldom a sense of a choice having been made or of ownership of emotional reactions and behaviors.

Borderline people often feel out of control. As they begin to develop the ability to "stop and think" *before* reacting, this new-found ability can gradually translate into an increased sense of self and self-control. They can begin to feel that they are more in charge of their own destinies.

Key to accomplishing this is acquiring the ability to pause for a moment. This can be accomplished in therapy sessions when the client tells the therapist about some upsetting event and experiences strong emotions in the moment. Therapists can choose to intervene at this point, interrupt, and encourage the client to "stop" for a moment, and then very directly suggest that the client should engage in some reality assessment and analytical thinking. (This technique is illustrated in a case example in the next section, "Challenging Cognitive Distortions.")

This kind of intervention attempts to halt escalating emotions and then to engage the person in using more logical thought processes to:

1. Make more accurate appraisals of the elements of distressing events

2. Gain realistic perspective, and

3. Engage in supportive self-talk

Challenging Cognitive Distortions

Almost always, during times of very intense emotional arousal, borderline people engage in the kind of thinking and inner perceiving that has been described by cognitive therapists as *cognitive distortions* or *negative self-talk*. Therapists must be alert to the need to notice the presence of distorted thinking, as revealed by the client's comments.

The most common cognitive distortions are listed in Table 8.1.

Table 8.1. Common Cognitive Distortions	
Cognitive Distortions	**Example**
All-or-none-thinking	"I am a complete failure." "He doesn't care about me at all."
Labeling	"I'm a stupid jerk." "She's an asshole."
Tunnel vision: seeing only the negative	"Absolutely nothing has gone right for me."
Negative predictions	"No one will ever love me." "My life will always be screwed up"
Arbitrary conclusions	"Everyone hates me."

Most of the time, people are unaware of such conclusions/thinking. It takes place at an unconscious or preconscious level. Their intense emotions are all that they notice. When these distortions are operating, they dramatically amplify emotional intensity. The strategy, within a session, is to interrupt the client, have him/her articulate inner thoughts, and help the client to engage in more accurate, realistic thinking. Let's look at a case example.

Case Example: Gail

Gail flew into a rage when her boyfriend showed up one hour late for a date. She broke dishes, cursed him, threw him out, and collapsed into despair, feeling flooded with suicidal thoughts. As she recounts this event in the therapy session, she again becomes very distraught. She trembles, weeps, and appears to be furious. Her feelings are escalating.

The therapist now has a choice point, and chooses to intervene.

Therapist: "Gail, I want to interrupt you for a minute. Please, just settle down for a moment. I know this is very upsetting . . . I want to ask you something. Right now while you are crying and feeling upset, what are you thinking? What's going through your mind?"

Gail: "Just that that son of a bitch says he loves me, but then he treats me like shit. He doesn't give a damn about me."

Therapist: "OK, what was it, in particular, that happened that made you think he was treating you like shit?"

Gail: "Forgetting our date, of course!"

Therapist: "Did he tell you why he was late?"

Gail: "Yeah, something about bad traffic or some other kind of lame excuse."

Therapist: "I want to know your opinion about something. OK?"

Gail: "What?"

Therapist: "You said he was treating you like shit . . . you felt upset about his being late. What I'd like to know is, have there been times when it was clear to you that he was treating you in a decent way? Has that ever happened?"

Gail: "Well yes." (She calms down somewhat.)

Therapist: "I know he was late this time and it really ticked you off. But, give
me an example of a time recently when he was good to you."

Gail: "Well, he did call the other day to ask me how my mom was doing. She had surgery last week, and he called me."

Therapist: "Again, I want your opinion. What did that mean to you when he called?"

Gail: "Well . . . that was pretty nice. He didn't have to call, but he did. I felt like he cared about me."

Therapist: "Have there been other times, too?"

Gail: "Oh, sure . . ."

Therapist: "Would it be accurate to say that even though he was late last night, that's not the whole story, that, in fact, there are times when he's been pretty decent to you?"

Gail: "That's true."

Therapist: "So that's true *and* you were upset that he was late last night?"

Gail: "Yes."

Therapist: "You tell me. When you stop and think about these other times when he's been good to you, do they matter to you? Does that make any difference at all?"

Gail: "It does, but I still don't like him to be late."

Therapist: "I hear that loud and clear."

Gail could have continued to fume about the event and in all likelihood it would have resulted in an increased sense of despair.

Note: It is standard practice in cognitive-behavioral (C-B) therapy for treating anxiety and depression to teach clients basic cognitive techniques, and encourage them to do C-B homework. Such strategies are often very successful. However, C-B techniques require some capacity to introspect, to reflect, and to discriminate inner experiences (e.g., to be able to distinguish between cognitions and emotions). Due to the borderline person's often chaotic thinking and information-processing, it may not be appropriate to *teach* C-B techniques early in therapy. Clients may not be able to practice it outside of therapy sessions. The therapist, however, during sessions when there is intense affective arousal, can use cognitive techniques as illustrated in the case example. These are used in the moment and can be very helpful with the therapist actively intervening. Later in treatment, many borderline clients may be better able to learn some C-B techniques, and, at that time, C-B homework may be appropriate.

Let's look at some specific elements of the therapist's intervention in the previous case example.

Elements of Successful Cognitive Intervention

- First, the therapist acknowledged that Gail was upset. Without this, it's not likely that she would be open to hearing anything else.

- Second, the therapist interrupts her; in a sense attempting to place a wedge between her run-away thinking and her escalating emotions.

- This was followed by more inquiry about what specifically happened that caused her to become so upset. The phrase "What was it in particular . . ." is a good way to help Gail shift the focus of her thinking and begin to look at the event in detail. The intent here is to move away from global precepts, to particulars. (This, in itself can often reduce arousal.)

- The therapist next inquired about what specific conclusions she was making about the event (i.e., she said, "he was treating me like shit . . . he doesn't give a damned about me"). This may be a distorted or exaggerated conclusion. The next step was to encourage her to broaden her perception to include not only the previous night, but the whole history of the relationship. She is especially focused on the single event, and has momentarily lost awareness of other realities, i.e., past interactions with her friend. The therapist, in a very direct way, pushes her to consider other relevant facts. Immersed in her emotions, she had been unable to do this for herself. The therapist steps in to help her do this.

Helpful Phrases

The phrases "I want to know your opinion" and "What did that mean to you?" are ways of acknowledging and strengthening Gail's self. Phrased this way, the therapist, in essence, says, "Your opinion matters to me" and it is also an invitation for her to use her own logical thought processes to reflect on the recent events. For the therapist to voice his or her opinion, rather than asking Gail for hers, takes the chance of infantilizing Gail. She has it in her to do this cognitive work; she simply needs help and encouragement to do it.

Cognitive Coping

This kind of intervention may occur many times during Gail's psychotherapy. In addition to it helping to contain and reduce arousal at the time it occurs in the therapy session, it can be gradually generalized to circumstances outside of the therapy sessions. The ability to learn this coping skill can be developed by repeated practice during sessions. Additionally, it can be framed and presented to the client in a very concrete way, as illustrated below. Let's assume that the intervention presented above did, in fact, result in Gail regaining a degree of emotional composure. If the timing is right, the therapist might continue in the following way:

Case Example:

Therapist: "Gail, I'd like to share something with you. I think something happened in the past few minutes that is important to think about. You had a very upsetting time last night and have continued to feel very distressed here today . . . What I did was to interrupt you, and you were able to stop yourself for a moment. You got enough control over your emotions in that moment so that you were able to step back a bit, and look more carefully at circumstances. Correct me if I'm wrong, but it seemed to me that when you did this, you calmed yourself down. You didn't seem as overwhelmed. Did you notice that?"

Gail: "Yes."

Therapist: "I think that maybe when you get in the middle of a lot of hurtful or upsetting feelings it's pretty easy to lose perspective. I think people do this a lot when their emotions are very strong . . . however, with just a little encouragement from me, you rather quickly were able to look at the situation from a different angle and then felt less upset. I think this can be a way for you to gain more control over your emotions. And, clearly, at the same time, you didn't deny your feelings. The fact remains that you were upset that he was late."

This may sound a bit like a lecture. The intent, however, is to make this cognitive process both more concrete and more conscious. We are intervening during the session and also starting to teach an important coping skill. If Gail is like most borderline people, she probably sees herself as generally being "out of control," "weak," and unable to deal with strong emotions. We want to help her to develop better skills for modulating her emotions. When this is successful, she'll not only be better able to regain control, she may also gradually come to see herself in a different light (e.g., "I can get upset, but I am able to control myself").

For the client, the take-home points from this mini-lecture are: When you have strong feelings, stop yourself, step back from the situation for a moment, and take stock of the circumstances by engaging in a more logical analysis of the facts (and especially the facts of the entire relationship, not just a single event). This is an active way to reduce emotional arousal and help yourself feel in better control.

The Sixty-Second Reality Check

To expand on this, it may be helpful to teach your clients how to do what I refer to as the *sixty-second reality check* (Preston, Varzos, and Liebert, 1997).

Tell them that when they begin to notice a strong emotional reaction, take a moment and go through the following steps.

The Sixty-Second Reality Check*

1. Take a deep breath, exhale, and silently count to ten.

2. Next, acknowledge that something upsetting has just happened and it probably touched an emotional chord. Say to yourself, "I want to get clear about this and keep a realistic perspective."

3. Then, ask yourself the following questions:

    a. Does this (what's just happened) really matter to me?

    b. In the grand scheme of things, how big a deal is it?

         Is it a true catastrophe?

         Is it likely to seem like a big deal in twenty-four hours?

         Is it likely to seem like a big deal in a week?

    c. Am I taking it personally?

    d. If I react now, will it:

         Probably be helpful?

         Probably make things worse?

    e. Would it make sense to take more time to think through the situation and then decide how to react?

    f. Are my thoughts and actions helping me or hurting me? What I am thinking or telling myself right now—is it helpful or is it hurtful?

---

* From *Make Every Session Count: Making the Most of Your Brief Therapy* © 1997 by John Preston, Nicolette Varzos and Douglas Liebert. New Harbinger Publications, Inc.

This exercise can be introduced and then practiced in therapy at times of strong emotional arousal. The client is also encouraged to try it in real-life circumstances. I recommend that a copy of the list be written out and given to clients so they can refer to it often.

When introducing this technique, two issues will either make it or break it. The first is that it is important to emphasize that the goal is not to cover up or deny true feelings. Clients have a legitimate right and need to be aware of their inner feelings. Rather, the goal is to help them turn down the volume on impulsive emotional reactions and to buy enough time so they can more successfully decide how they want to respond.

The second issue is that the technique may be difficult to use if the emotions of the moment are extremely intense. This is why they need to practice spotting emotional arousal early (before it escalates). It may also be necessary to take a "time-out." Time-out involves removing oneself from the immediate situation. If it's during a phone call, the person may find it helpful to learn how to say, "I'm pretty upset right now. I want to cool off a bit (or take a break). Let me call you back in five minutes." If the interaction is face-to-face, it is very helpful to leave the room and go outside or take a walk around the block. After there is a bit of decreased intensity, the person is much more likely to be able to use the sixty-second reality check.

As with any new skill, this will take a lot of practice and this is where the therapist must provide a great deal of support and encouragement.

An assumption underlying this approach is that BPD clients are exceptionally emotionally sensitive. This is just how it is and this is accepted. We are not asking them to somehow alter their inner level of sensitivity, nor are we being critical of them. Rather, this approach assumes that extreme sensitivity is a given. Our intent is to help borderline clients develop coping strategies designed to reduce the negative consequences of this exquisite sensitivity.

Scaling

If you carefully observe statements made in the heat of strong feelings, most involve conclusions or predictions that are unrealistically extreme, such as "I am *completely* overwhelmed," "He is *absolutely* wrong!" "I hate her fucking guts." "I am *never* going to be treated decently." These statements are absolutes ... 100 percent, black-and-white statements. Another very helpful strategy for improving cognitive processing and reality testing is to teach borderline patients how to use scaling.

With scaling, every time clients describe other people, stressful events, or their own feelings, they are encouraged to rate the level of intensity they feel or accuracy of the statement on a scale from one to ten (one being minimal, and ten being a lot). For example, Jim states, "I can't trust her at all." The therapist might say, "Let me ask you about that, Jim. Are you saying she is one hundred percent untrustworthy? On a scale of one to ten, how untrustworthy do you think she is?" Or Betty says, "That bastard doesn't give a damn about me!" and the therapist inquires, "Is this a matter of him not caring *one* bit? Never caring at all? What do you say, Betty, on a scale from one to ten how uncaring do you really believe Doug is?"

Some clients might say, "Last night he was a ten." Then, the intervention could shift to "Maybe that was true for last night. But, consider the entire history of your relationship—not just last night. How would you rate Doug, overall?" Betty says, "Oh, probably a four or a five." Therapist, "So, overall, a four or a five, *and* last night he scored a ten. Right?"

Emphasis is placed on the word *and.* This is intentional. It is designed to help the client move away from black-or-white categorical thinking and to consider the complexity of events or relationships. When a person says, "Overall a four or a five, *but* last night he was a ten," there is a strong tendency for the word "but" to have the effect of negating the earlier statement and we are once again left with an all-or-none conclusion. Additionally, this approach is effective in that it allows people to express and acknowledge how they feel about specific events (and feel validated) while at the same time, broadening their perspective and improving the accuracy of their perceptions and conclusions. I want to emphasize that this is not just a matter of semantics. In a very real way, encouraging the use of "and statements" is a powerful way to influence cognition in the moment. Furthermore, if it is done frequently, clients can learn to do it on their own.

Auxiliary Reality Testing

Several interventions are used to help enhance the patient's ability to perceive reality accurately. The intent is to help the client see things more clearly. I will discuss two types of interventions that involve what some authors have called *auxiliary reality testing.* The first intervention is designed to correct transference distortions.

Transference Reactions

Transference reactions occur during the psychotherapy of many, if not most, clients. They are characterized by a significant distortion in the perception of the therapist, and a resulting strong emotional response. An example of this might be the client who suddenly feels a heightened sense of shame, and is unable to make eye contact with the therapist. He reports feeling worried that the therapist will criticize or humiliate him, despite the fact that there have been no instances of this ever having occurred during treatment.

Presumably, this belief and fear is a function of the client's history of relationships where he was, in fact, the recipient of considerable criticism and shaming. In a powerful way, his early experiences have left their mark by way of enduring cognitive schemas. Such schemas operate to influence and bias ongoing perceptions and expectations.

As mentioned earlier, higher-level functioning clients usually recognize the inappropriateness of transference feelings (i.e., they can appreciate that their reactions are not in keeping with the reality of the therapist's behavior or the history of the therapeutic relationship). Borderline clients often react to these feelings as if they are realistic and justified.

A time-honored approach for dealing with transference reactions is to explore the meaning of the feelings in the hope of understanding more about the underlying dynamics. Thus, a therapist might respond to the client, "Can you tell me more about how you are feeling? What's going through your mind just now?" This intervention is designed to intensify the emotion and to encourage increased awareness. With neurotics, this can be a high-yield intervention. It may help the client and therapist alike to understand more clearly the nature of the person's inner sense of shame and his fear of being humiliated by others. However, exploring or interpreting the transference can be risky with borderline patients. It can have the effect of greatly intensifying the underlying emotions and lead to further destabilization.

Challenging Transference Distortions

With borderline clients, it is often advisable to directly challenge or correct transference distortions as they occur. Let's illustrate this with some examples:

> **Case Example:** "I wonder if you are misinterpreting something. You are acting as if I am going to criticize or shame you, but I want you to know that I have no intention of doing so. In fact, and please think about this, I don't believe that I have ever acted towards you in any way that would shame you. . . . What are your thoughts about that?" or, "Jerry, I know you've experienced a lot of criticism and shaming from your father. We've talked about that a lot. I think that in some way you may be reacting to me, just now, as if I were like your father. But, I am not your father, and I have no intention of being critical, or shaming you."

In these interventions, the therapist is doing the reality testing for his client. This is a very directive way to improve the accuracy of the patient's perceptions, which most of the time has the effect of reducing the intensity of transference reactions. An additional comment can also be helpful.

> "Jerry, you and I both know how hard it was for you, growing up with your father's judgmental harshness. I just want you to know that I understand that you might anticipate that others would treat you in a similar way. I don't blame you at all for watching out for that. But I do want to make it very clear that I have no intention of treating you that way."

Related to the issue of transference distortions are the phenomena of overidealization and devaluation.

Overidealized Transference

As mentioned previously, it is very common for borderline clients to rapidly develop overidealized transferences. It might be momentarily gratifying for a therapist to bask in the glow of "You're the best therapist in the world!"—but watch out! Almost always, such overidealization rapidly turns into hostility and devaluation as the client experiences the inevitable truth that the therapist is not 100 percent wonderful, nurturing, empathic, etc.

One way to counter this is to tactfully present the client with reality, for example:

Therapist: "You are seeing me as being an especially great therapist. I'm glad you feel positive about therapy, but I want to talk to you about something. Have you ever had times when you thought very highly of someone, only to discover that they had some faults and weren't so great after all."

Client: "Many times."

Therapist: "Well, it could happen here, too. And my guess is that if you see me as wonderful or perfect, it could be a tremendous disappointment to you to find out that I also have faults or that I can also make mistakes. I want to assure you that I'll do my best to be a good therapist. But it might be a good idea for you to keep in mind that I'm not perfect."

This is a way to help clients anticipate a situation that might otherwise result in profound disappointment. It is a way of enhancing their reality-testing abilities, of showing your concern so they do not get hurt in therapy, and of simply being honest.

It should be noted, however, that at times, an idealizing transference may be important to the client. It may be one element, especially early in treatment, that helps to inspire and maintain hope. Thus, it is important to approach this issue gingerly and with great sensitivity.

Reality Testing

From time to time, everyone jumps to conclusions and makes erroneous assumptions based on scant data. One version of this is what Burns (1980) refers to as "mind reading." Let's illustrate this with an example. A client arrived at work, and said hello to a coworker who seemed to ignore him. He concluded, "She hates me." This conclusion may be accurate, but it is also possible that there were many other reasons she failed to respond. For example, she may have been very preoccupied, worrying about her own problems. With mind reading, the person arrives at a conclusion and believes it is absolutely a fact, without checking it out with the other person.

We often hear our clients make all sorts of unwarranted assumptions and conclusions. Rather than accepting these conclusions as factual, it is important to inquire. For example:

"Robert, I really wonder if you might have been jumping to conclusions. Maybe she doesn't like you. That's possible, but it seems to me there may be a lot of other reasons she didn't respond. Maybe she was just very preoccupied or so busy she didn't hear you?" or,

"Well maybe she doesn't like you. But let me ask you, have there been other times in the past when she said or did things that made it look as if she was friendly towards you?" or, a third possible intervention:

"Robert, maybe it's true that she doesn't like you. But I want to ask you, how can you absolutely know what she's feeling without talking to her? Things have been difficult for you, especially recently, and you sure don't need any more unpleasant feelings at this time. I'm concerned that if you simply assume that she doesn't like you and you don't check it out with her, that you'll end up just feeling worse. Maybe she was just preoccupied. How can you really know. . . . What do you think about what I've been saying?"

The goal is not only to intervene during therapy sessions, but to help patients see that they may be jumping to erroneous conclusions a good deal of the time, and to suggest that they try to be more cognizant of this. At some point they will begin to ask, "Am I jumping to conclusions?" on their own. A more careful analysis of the facts is what reality testing is all about.

Spotting and Avoiding Toxic Interactions

It is amazing how many borderline people jump from the frying pan into the fire apparently unaware that certain relationships are high risks for disaster. One way to understand this is that emotional needs of the moment may compel impulsive actions (e.g., quick involvement in a sexual relationship). Often, there are multiple signs of potential danger that go unnoticed, for example, a woman might feel a sudden strong attraction to a man who has been married five times and is an alcoholic. She rapidly concludes "I have met Mr. Right," or a man who has a history of being terribly emotionally abused by his mother continues to visit her regularly, still hoping to receive love from her despite always having been rejected and hurt.

An important way therapists can intervene with these types of problems is to help the client realize that certain situations or particular relationships are toxic, and to keep this clearly in mind. It is often wise for our clients to learn to avoid such interactions much in the same way that people with ulcers learn to avoid spicy foods.

More psychodynamically oriented therapists may argue that it is better to attempt a working-through of the underlying dynamics that propel people back into these noxious relationships (i.e., the repetition compulsion). However, it is generally not realistic to undertake that process in briefer therapy for severe personality disorders. What may be achievable is for the person to develop a better sense about what kinds of relationships are likely to be hurtful, and then to make more informed choices either to approach or to avoid. It's not our job to tell them what to do, but it is important to encourage our clients to open their eyes, gather data, and be more thoughtful before leaping into situations that are at high risk for disappointment and emotional pain.

Developing Abilities to Experience and Express Emotions

Although most borderline individuals are characterized as being "too emotional" owing to their frequent episodes of dyscontrol, it is also important to appreciate that much of the time, they are in states of overcontrol and excessive avoidance of emotions. Many borderline people grew up in families in which normal emotional expressions were either prohibited or subject to intense punishment, criticism, and shaming. Often, when important and painful emotions did surface, this was greeted with marked invalidation. Thus, on countless occasions these kids had to find ways to massively inhibit their emotional expressions. As a result, most borderline people grew up without being able to learn or practice appropriate ways of experiencing and expressing the full range of human emotions.

As adults, these people come to us, in a sense, with primarily two emotional difficulties. The first is the tendency for extremely maladaptive emotional dyscontrol. The second, paradoxically, is the tendency toward overcontainment and poorly developed abilities to express legitimate inner feelings. Like all human beings, borderline people face losses, disappointments, abuse by others, and so forth, and they too need ways to mourn losses, to work through painful feelings, and to appropriately express anger, frustration, etc. Thus, although many therapeutic interventions are directed towards managing emotional dyscontrol, it is also very important to find ways to help our BPD clients access, experience, and express feelings in adaptive ways. In fact, as they begin to find more adaptive outlets for emotional expression, this, in itself, may reduce the frequency of dyscontrol.

With that goal in mind, there are three ingredients that we will consider.

1. To acknowledge feelings as understandable and legitimate.

2. To reduce secondary/unnecessary pain and suffering.

3. To understand that ultimately some deep pain must be expressed in order for growth and healing to take place.

Acknowledging Feelings as Legitimate

The first of these goals is the importance of conveying to our clients that it is understandable, appropriate, legitimate, and ultimately *necessary* for people to acknowledge certain inner painful feelings. This can, of course, be done in a direct and verbal way during treatment sessions, as feelings arise. However, probably more important are the subtle nonverbal communications that occur in the context of the patient-therapist relationship.

These clients are primed to expect others to respond to their emotions by withdrawing, criticizing, shaming, looking disgusted, or by counterattack. The therapist's response to their emotional expressions can make a significant difference. A stance that includes neutrality (i.e., nonjudgmental) and a clear communication of caring and respect are likely to create a new, corrective experience for the client eventually. To not be shamed, not be slammed, not be ridiculed . . . by the therapist often stands out as a singular experience for a borderline client. Implicit in the therapist's response are messages such as "Your feelings matter . . . they are legitimate . . . they are to be honored . . . I want to understand." This requires a careful balancing act in which the therapist may simultaneously communicate "These emotions are legitimate" *and* "we need to find a more adaptive, less extreme way for you to express them."

Reducing Secondary/Unnecessary Pain

In regard to the second ingredient, we frequently see that primary emotional experiences are accompanied by secondary feelings that greatly intensify personal suffering. Most secondary feelings are a consequence of marked self-criticism. Let's consider some examples:

- A man's mother dies. Beyond significant grief, he also thinks frequently, "I was a terrible son . . . I didn't spend enough time with her . . . I hate myself."

- A woman's romantic relationship ends. Much of her pain stems from her conviction, "No wonder he left me, I'm such a loser, I'm so boring, so stupid, so ugly."

- A young man feels deeply shamed and humiliated after breaking down crying upon receiving a rejection from a potential employer. "What the hell is wrong with me? I'm just a weak, sniveling crybaby."

An important aspect of psychotherapy with all types of clients, is to help patients sort out the sources of their despair; especially helping them to make the distinction between what some call "necessary" and "unnecessary pain" (Peck 1978; Johnson 1985; Preston 1993). Necessary pain is the emotional suffering that is inevitable, as all human beings must encounter significant losses, rejections, disappointments, and frustrations by virtue of their humanity. These are basic, honest experiences of sadness, anger, fear, and distress. They are necessary in two respects. First, they are ultimately unavoidable. (If you get cut, you will bleed. Similarly, on some inner level, primary emotions are automatically elicited in certain situations.) Second, the expression of basic emotions is a crucial aspect of emotional healing and growth.

In contrast, unnecessary pain largely stems from the aforementioned tendency for harsh self-criticism. Most of our neurotic clients are dominated by such unnecessary pain, so it certainly is not unique to BPD. However, the critical self-judgments of borderline clients can be especially intense.

One way to address this is to share the concept of necessary and unnecessary pain with clients and to illustrate it by making reference to specific ways this has been manifested in what they have said during sessions. Then, it may be helpful to flag these kind of statements *as they occur*; to point them out *in the moment* to help clients become more aware of their tendency to self-judge. (It is remarkable how often borderline people make statements revealing harsh self-judgment.) Simply noting this within sessions, in itself, is an intervention that may begin to chip away at the more automatic quality of their self-criticism.

Beyond this, it may be productive to have clients take a closer look at what they are saying and to challenge their conclusions. Let's look at one example:

Client: "What the hell is wrong with me?! I'm just a weak, sniveling crybaby."

Therapist: "Tom, you're being pretty hard on yourself. I want to ask you something. We both know you have had a lot of difficulty landing a job. I also know that you felt very hopeful about this particular job opportunity. You really had your heart set on it. Please, tell me . . . given how important this was to you, is it understandable to you that you would have very strong feelings of disappointment when you found out you didn't get it?"

This style of question often helps the person to shift away from extreme negative self-judgment into a more realistic and more compassionate frame of reference. And, of course, what also comes through is the implicit message from the therapist, that the pain *is* understandable.

When the time is right, it may also be helpful to state very directly, "You are pretty damned hard on yourself. I think your self-criticism just causes more hurt, and doesn't help at all. If at all possible, I want to encourage you to really work at developing a more compassionate way of treating yourself."

Unavoidable Pain

The third and final ingredient is communicating to our clients a message that conveys the following belief or assumption: "Some pain simply is not avoidable and it must be felt and somehow endured," and "there may be ways to learn how to do this." Another message is that the therapist has confidence that the client can do this, at least to some degree. This takes us to the last set of interventions for coping with intense emotional arousal.

Marsha Linehan has addressed this issue well. She refers to this as "learning to bear pain skillfully." (The reader is referred to her excellent text for more details (1993).) How do people endure painful times when the situation cannot be changed? Let's look at some strategies.

Strategies for Bearing Emotional Pain

I. **Developing the ability to accept life as it is in the moment of emotional pain.** This involves the capacity or choice to refrain from insisting "it shouldn't be," and to accept this simply as the reality of the moment. This certainly does not mean that you deny the unpleasantness, nor does it represent passivity. "I don't have to like this, but at this moment, it simply is the truth" (This concept is also recommended in the work of Jon Kabat-Zinn (1995).)

2. **Engaging in nondestructive distractions.** This includes: physically leaving a situation and engaging in activities (e.g., one of my clients would go into her yard and dig holes, another would play an action-packed video game), physical exercise, etc.

3. **Altering arousal and bodily response.** For example, taking a hot bath, stretching, vigorous exercise, curling up with a warm blanket, breathing exercises, walking, rocking, using relaxation techniques.

4. **Going to a place you have created that is pleasant, safe, and private.** For example, Jill decided to make a special corner of her backyard into a place of escape, safety, and beauty. She planted some flowers, made a small rock garden, and purchased a comfortable wooden chair. At times of distress, she told her family that she needed a bit of alone time, and went to her garden retreat.

5. **Attempting to find meaning in the pain.** For example, a young man who lost his father would often remind himself at times of intense grief, "One reason it hurts so much is because I loved him. My grief is a reminder of the closeness I felt with my Dad."

6. **Using compassionate and nurturing self-talk.** For example, "I need to be gentle with myself . . ." "I'm a decent person and I deserve to be good to myself, especially during painful times." This also includes avoiding negative self-talk such as "I don't deserve to feel better" or "I am a bad person."

7. **Maintaining realistic perspective.** For example, "I am very sad now, but I know from past experience that this sadness won't last forever. Very likely I'll feel at least a little better tomorrow" or "I know that panic attacks feel awful, but I also know that they last only a few minutes. Just hang on. This should subside soon."

8. **Using grounding techniques.** (These are discussed in Chapter 7 in the section "Focus and Stabilization.")

Typically, BPD patients have had repeated experiences of feeling overwhelmed and unable to cope at times of distress. The experience of total powerlessness always markedly intensifies emotional pain. As we work with our clients on developing better distress tolerance skills, they will gradually acquire a greater sense of confidence. Then, emotional pain will not always have to be avoided.

DEVELOPING PROBLEM-SOLVING SKILLS

Poor decisions and impulse-driven actions, especially in the context of interpersonal relationships, often create tremendous chaos in the lives of borderline people. It is often volatile, impulsive behavior that contributes significantly to ruptures in relationships and to occupational instability. A major goal in treatment is to help the person engage in more effective problem solving. This constitutes a lot of the work done in therapy sessions, which hopefully will translate into the acquisition of more adaptive coping skills.

Often, a chain of reactions can be identified. (See Figure 8.1.)

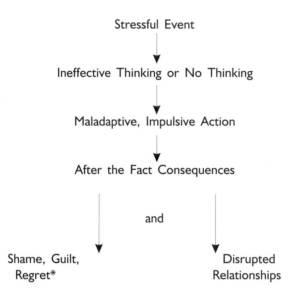

* These secondary emotional reactions are often a source of tremendous personal suffering for the BPD client.

Figure 8.1. Impulse-Ridden Chain of Reactions

One sign of ego strength is the capacity when upset to control action long enough to engage in adaptive information-processing (which includes perceiving the situation accurately, maintaining a realistic perceptive, planning for action, and anticipating consequences). This is exactly what most borderline patients cannot do in the heat of an emotionally aroused moment.

More adaptive problem solving can be taught, modeled, and practiced during therapy sessions as clients begin to share with the therapist recent distressing experiences. Linehan (1993) describes several important steps in this process.

Steps for Adaptive Problem Solving

1. Time-out (as mentioned previously) may involve having the person, at the first sign of escalating emotion, go to another room or go outside (to create distance between self and other). I've suggested to clients that as they notice

increasing feelings of distress, to touch their wristwatch as a concrete cue to take a "time-out." This allows for the slight pause (discussed in Chapter 3 and described earlier in this chapter in the section "Stop and Think") and greatly increases the chance that they can then engage in some type of cognitive activity.

2.   Linehan suggests that clients then attend to and observe what just happened in the moments leading up to the distress. In doing so, the client should try to approach this with a "just the facts" perspective, i.e., stick to concrete events, and observable behaviors, and avoid the tendency to infer others' motives, feelings, or intentions.

3.   Next, describe *in words*, exactly what happened. Clients should describe environmental, behavioral, and interpersonal events, in a step-by-step fashion. Many clients will provide only the "headlines" but it is important to slow them down, and ask for lots of details. This is an important element, because in order to articulate details and to verbalize the event it is necessary to engage more conscious thought processes (a critical ingredient missing in moments of impulsivity). Practicing this over and over again in therapy sessions helps to develop this ability so that in real-life circumstances this strategy can be applied more readily. These moments of thinking and reflecting create a wedge between arousal and impulsive action. It also allows time to evaluate the situation, options, and consequences more critically.

4.   A potent way to reduce emotional intensity is to make a distinction between "wants" and "shoulds." Often in the intensity of the moment, there are underlying cognitions based largely on a particular type of insistence: "It *should* be a certain way!" This may take many forms, such as

- He shouldn't do that!

- I shouldn't be so upset!

- It shouldn't turn out like this!

At the heart of these thoughts is a desperate kind of insistence and an unspoken assumption that if things are not a certain way, then *everything* will be overwhelmingly bad (catastrophic thinking). In a powerful way this cognition can turn up the volume significantly on a host of unpleasant emotions.

One way to counter this is to encourage the client, to rephrase the thought in terms of "what I *want*" rather than how it should be. For example:

- I don't want him to do that.

- I don't want to feel so upset, but I do.

- I don't want it to turn out this way, and it has, and I don't like it.

- I want her to know how I like to be treated.

Doing this can reduce emotional arousal without negating the person's inner feelings or desires. With a decrease in arousal, people are in a much better position to engage in logical thinking and problem solving.

5. Get clear about desired outcomes.

6. Think about specific actions you can take.

7. Evaluate likely consequences.

Linehan emphasizes that throughout this process, the client should simultaneously consider three objectives:

1. Specific, desired, concrete outcomes

2. Maintaining (not destroying) the relationship, and

3. Preserving self-respect

Borderline people often get locked into insisting that things should be fair or right. Linehan (1993) recommends that we encourage them to focus less on issues of right and wrong and more on "doing what works" or "taking action that in the long run will help me and not harm me."

The net gain in learning this problem-solving strategy, ultimately, is feeling more in control of oneself. It can reduce the frequency and intensity of impulsive behavior. It can also lead to actions or reactions that are likely to be more adaptive.

CHAPTER 9

Self-Destructive Behavior

In this chapter we will discuss interventions that focus on alleviating self-destructive behavior. This includes suicidal and what some have called para-suicidal behavior (i.e., self-mutilations and nonlethal suicide gestures). It is important to note that although some clients do exhibit both suicidal and para-suicidal symptoms, these behaviors are not necessarily related and, in fact, may stem from quite different underlying motivations. Let's consider this issue in more detail.

SELF-MUTILATION

When therapists inquire about the subjective experience just prior to and during episodes of self-mutilation, two types of responses are often given. The most common is that the patient had been in a state of tremendous emotional distress (often described as "intolerable"). At the moment of self-harm, the person felt some sense of relief from that "intolerable stress" (e.g., calmer; "I felt it let off steam"). This was the desired outcome. Many lay people assume that burning or cutting yourself must be associated with a desire to inflict pain or self-punishment. The motives reported by many BPD clients, however, are quite the opposite. The aim is to *reduce* suffering. The self-mutilation results in a marked diminution of psychic pain, and this self-soothing motive must be understood by therapists (Liebenluft et al. 1987). The following case examples illustrate this need to reduce emotional suffering by the infliction of physical pain.

Case Examples

Mr. V. was referred by his primary care doctor. The physician had evaluated him for problems with rectal bleeding, for which he could identify no medical cause. The doctor had always thought Mr. V. had peculiar affect and seemed "disturbed." After a few sessions with a therapist, it was learned that Mr. V., when feeling extremely upset, felt the urge to hurt himself. He did so by placing a piece of a razor blade into a pencil eraser, and then inserting the eraser into his rectum. He stated that when he did this he felt "cleaner." He also said that he often felt extremely guilty and that this form of self-harm somehow seemed appropriate as a type of punishment that he deserved.

Ms. R. had been awarded "teacher of the year" three times in the past five years. She was referred by her school principal when one day it was discovered that she was injecting her hand with a syringe in her classroom after school. Ms. R. told her principal that she was not using drugs; rather, she was injecting small amounts of battery acid beneath her skin.

When seen by the therapist, Ms. R. stated that she often felt intense panic feelings and a kind of "seething rage," and that she was somehow able to contain these feelings during school hours. However, as soon as the children left, she frequently would engage in some form of self-mutilation. She then revealed the upper inner parts of her forearms, which were covered with dozens of cigarette burns.

Neurobiology of Self-Mutilation

There is a good deal of speculation regarding the neurobiology of BPD as this relates to the phenomenon of self-harm. Some evidence indicates that for borderline people there is an acquired biologic capacity to evoke large releases of endogenous opiates (endorphins) by provoking rather minor injury (Russ et al. 1992; Kemperman et al. 1997).

Note: Many humans will release massive amounts of endorphins following a very severe injury, such as a traumatic amputation. The result is one to two hours of analgesia and remarkably little subjective pain, given the seriousness of the injury. However, for most of us, a razor blade cut or a cigarette burn on the arm is simply not severe enough to evoke endorphin release; there is no sense of relief, it just hurts.

This odd biological response is also seen in monkeys that have been raised under conditions of severe neglect during infancy. Marked deprivation of nurturing (and tactile-kinesthetic stimulation ordinarily provided by hugging, holding, and rocking) likely affects early brain development; in particular an abnormal development of the opiate system. One result is that these seriously neglected monkeys, later in life, like our borderline clients, will, when under considerable stress, engage in self-mutilation.

Numbness

Another, although somewhat less common reason for self-injury (especially cutting) is that at the moment of pain or seeing blood, the person feels reassured that he/she is, indeed, alive. Generally, the precursor to the self-harm was a state of profound numbness, dissociation, derealization, or emptiness. Again, the desired outcome basically is not self-harm, but rather a sense of reassurance and relief.

On one level, of course we want our clients to take action to reduce emotional suffering. However, there are serious risks to self-mutilation, such as the following:

- It can sometimes result in accidental death.

- It can lead to medical complications such as infection.

- It can leave hideous scars and deformities.

- It can contribute to the borderline person's sense of shame or conviction that he/she is "crazy."

The most effective strategies for reducing self-mutilation ultimately involve helping the BPD client acquire more adaptive ways either to endure or to reduce emotional arousal. When these are effective, self-mutilation is less likely to occur. Beyond this, however, there are approaches aimed more directly at reducing self-harm.

REDUCING SELF-HARM

An important starting point is to explore the client's subjective experiences leading up to and during self-injury behaviors. The intent is to understand motives and outcomes, and then to share that understanding with the patient. A compassionate and nonjudgmental stance is essential. Most borderline people have had the experience of others responding to accounts of self-mutilation with revulsion, disgust, and critical remarks, e.g., "Are you nuts?, " "God, why in the hell are you doing this to yourself?" As therapists, we want to support their general desire to reduce emotional pain (which is essentially a healthy motive) and at the same time encourage them to find less dangerous ways of reaching that goal.

Simply reframing the mutilating acts as a form of self-care or a behavior motivated by the desire to reduce suffering can be helpful. That is, if the message is conveyed to the client that the therapist understands the primary goal of the self-harm was the reduction of emotional pain, then the client may be better able to view himself/herself in a less pathological light.

Strategies to Reduce Self-Harm

After addressing motives we can next select one of three main strategies for decreasing self-mutilating behavior. The first is *limit setting*. For example, the therapist might say,

Case Example: "Carol, I certainly don't blame you for wanting to cut yourself at those times when you feel so overwhelmed. It sounds as if you know this will provide some immediate relief. But, I want to be very clear with you. Ultimately, cutting yourself is risky and dangerous and I don't think it's a good solution. The next time you feel the urge to cut yourself, you need to stop yourself. We need to figure out less dangerous things for you to do at those times, but first and foremost, you must not cut yourself."

Or in another example, during a therapy session the client becomes very upset and begins to dig his fingernails into his arm, drawing blood. The therapist might say,

Case Example: "Mike, I know you are very upset, but you must stop hurting yourself immediately. You have to control yourself." The therapist may need to insist that if the client does not stop, that the therapist will end the session. "It may be difficult, but I believe that you can find a way to stop hurting yourself. And if you do not stop right now, then I will have to insist that we end the session. I cannot permit you to keep doing this."

Telling a client to stop self-mutilating behavior, especially outside the treatment setting, may sound a bit ludicrous, at first. However, BPD clients often develop strong attachments to their therapists and this gives the treater some leverage. Such requests often work to help patients muster better control, especially if the request is delivered with compassion and in the context of understanding.

A second approach is to encourage clients at times of intense emotional distress to engage in nondestructive actions that will serve to distract them or to reduce physiologic arousal. (Vigorous exercise is especially helpful because in itself it may produce some elevation of serotonin and endorphin levels in the brain.)

The third and final approach should be limited to those times when other strategies fail and when self-mutilating behavior is inevitable. The client can be taught that there are less dangerous ways to evoke the release of endorphins (thus achieving similar results to the relief obtained after a cutting or burning episode). One method is to hold ice cubes in their hands, until the cold begins to hurt (Steve Hallon in Linehan, 1993b, p98). Another method is to place a rubber band on the wrist and pop it hard several times. (Trust me, this does hurt.) A third strategy is to fill a bucket or a sink with water and ice cubes and immerse a hand in it, keeping it there until it hurts; thus evoking an endorphin rush. These ways of inducing pain are much less likely to result in physical harm and do not create lasting scars.

For this third method to be effective, attention must be given to how it is presented. First, you will need to provide a mini-lecture regarding the role of physical pain and endorphins and explain why self-injury results in *transient* relief from emotional pain. Second, it must be emphasized that your intention is *not* to encourage such clients to harm themselves. Rather, it is a last-ditch strategy for reducing overwhelming emotions, if other approaches have proven to be ineffective.

SUICIDAL BEHAVIOR

Interestingly, in most cases of self-mutilation, the behavior and resulting scars are well-kept secrets. Many borderline people feel ashamed of these behaviors, and their self-destructive actions carry no interpersonal/manipulative implications. In contrast, some suicidal behaviors are motivated by a very strong desire to influence others (e.g., to induce guilt, to recruit help, or to punish). The suicide attempts are revealed publicly and how others respond makes a difference. Driven by intense neediness or fears of abandonment, many borderline people will make suicidal threats or gestures. (The motives may be conscious and intentional or largely unconscious.) Often, such behaviors are quite impulsive.

Threats and Manipulation

When dealing with suicidal threats and gestures, the therapist must be careful not to unwittingly be drawn into response patterns that reinforce the behavior. Desperate pleas for help can be punctuated by suicidal threats and will elicit prompt responses from psychotherapists. If suicidal talk results in phone calls that are returned more quickly, longer sessions, or a greater air of concern, such behaviors can become powerfully reinforced.

Strategies for Addressing Suicidal Behavior

The starting point when dealing with these behaviors is in uncovering, understanding, and acknowledging the client's legitimate feelings of loneliness, neediness, or fear of abandonment. The more these feelings can be expressed outwardly in words, the less likely they will be manifested in suicidal behavior. We might suggest to the patient that these feelings or needs are very important and that we need to work together to find more effective ways of expressing and dealing with them.

When suicidal impulses are verbalized, it is important to express appropriate concern (taking it seriously) but without being overly solicitous. This involves being firm regarding the "frame," i.e., not allowing sessions to extend beyond regular stopping times, except under unusual circumstances. This can be a balancing act because the therapist must, on the one hand, not play into these behaviors too much (thus reinforcing them), and, on the other hand, maintain a careful watchfulness for the emergence of more serious suicidal ideations. I often relate to patients some version of the following statement:

Case Example: "You and I both know that if a person is 100 percent intent on killing himself, he'll do it. I know you've felt suicidal and I take that very seriously. My goal in working with you is for us to figure out better ways for you to cope during the times you feel overwhelmed, so you don't have to resort to suicide. I feel confident that we can do this."

Suicide Rate For BPD: Lifetime Risk

- 7.6 percent of BPD patients die by suicide.

- Most borderline suicides occur during the first decade of the illness.

- Suicides dramatically drop off after the age of thirty.

Sources: Stone (1987); Gabbard (1996)

- Predictors of greater risk of suicide include: co-morbid major depression, a history of serious prior attempt(s), and substance abuse.

Source: Brodsky and Mann (1997)

By expressing the fact that people can and do kill themselves, in a very real sense, the therapist is saying that, ultimately, it is the client's choice (which can somewhat reduce the role of the therapist as "rescuer"). It also conveys a confident message that other alternatives can be developed.

Therapists can go on to say that they count on the patient to bring up any suicidal concerns during sessions. And in the event that patients feel a strong urge to kill themselves, it is necessary that they get themselves to an emergency room or psychiatric inpatient facility.

Certainly there are times in which borderline clients present with high-risk suicidal impulses. These must be taken very seriously indeed and addressed by way of telephone calls, more frequent sessions, and/or hospitalization. Making a clear distinction between manipulative threats and lethal intent is, unfortunately, not always easy to do.

WHEN INTERVENTION DOESN'T WORK

Sometimes, despite even heroic efforts, patients self-destruct. Occasionally this can be traced to mismanaged treatment. However, more often it is because we have taken on a case from Hell. Some borderline people enter treatment with god-awful histories. I tell my students that to take on such clients is akin to trying to stop a run-away train at the bottom of a mountain. It has picked up so much speed on the way down that it is impossible to stop. Many borderline people have had decades of terrible suffering and nothing short of an act of God could steer them from their disastrous course. You can rationalize that such events come with the territory. However, in my experience, this notion has provided very little consolation value to colleagues who have had a suicide in their practice.

If and when a suicide occurs, it behooves all of us to take a close look at what we have done (or failed to do) in treatment. Sometimes mistakes are made. Sometimes even very good therapists have been seduced into doing interventions in the treatment of borderline patients that go against their better judgment. And, ultimately, in the aftermath of a suicide, the therapist must seek out support and find acceptance and forgiveness for the fact that we too are only human.

CHAPTER 10

Psychopharmacology

The appropriate use of selected psychotropic medications can greatly facilitate the treatment of borderline clients. Although many clinicians have had experience in treating BPD with psychiatric medications, currently, well-controlled research studies are limited. A number of existing studies have methodological flaws. In particular, one common problem has been the lumping together of all sorts of borderline clients into large treatment groups and not taking into account co-morbid Axis I disorders.

In evaluating clinical outcomes in studies of psychopharmacology, it is helpful to delineate three subgroups of borderline patients. These subgroups have been derived both by research methods (cluster and factor analysis) and by a method that psychopharmacologist Donald Klein calls "pharmacological behavioral dissection." This latter approach looks at how different groups of patients respond to psychotropic mediations; and based on their response patterns, the following subtypes have been identified.

HYSTEROID-DYSPHORIC

These borderline clients present with a significant degree of emotional liability and are exquisitely sensitive to interpersonal rejection, loss, and abandonment. As a consequence, they often cannot tolerate being alone and may engage in desperate attempts to maintain attachments, including clinging behavior and manipulative suicidal threats or gestures. These patients are at great risk for recurring depression.

SCHIZOTYPAL

These borderline patients chronically display odd thinking, ideas of reference, magical thinking, vagueness, very idiosyncratic beliefs, and, periodically, they experience marked episodes of depersonalization or derealization and transient psychoses. As mentioned in the chapter on diagnosis, such people likely represent a truer sort of borderline schizophrenia.

ANGRY-IMPULSIVE

These people are characterized by their pervasively hostile-aggressive way of interacting with others. They have very low frustration tolerance and can be quite volatile. As a result, their interpersonal relations are replete either with ongoing intense friction or multiple rejections.

In addition to these subtypes, it is important to keep in mind that many, if not most, borderline personalities have co-morbid Axis I disorders—major depression and substance abuse are especially common. These coexisting disorders always complicate the picture and must be dealt with in any treatment approach. Clearly, it is essential to treat major depression, bipolar disorder, and panic disorder with appropriate psychotropic medications.

TREATMENT OPTIONS

No medication can directly treat personality disorders, per se. Rather, psychotropic medications are used to ameliorate certain target symptoms. The results of the limited studies available would indicate that the medications of choice are those listed in Table 10.1. A reduction in target symptoms can contribute significantly to improved coping ability and reduced levels of emotional despair. Reduced effect intensity can set the stage for more effective cognitive processing and reality testing. Additionally, decreases in irritability, intense clinging, desperate neediness, and related behaviors often result in a noticeable decrease in interpersonal friction. As the quality of their relationships improves, many borderline people begin to feel more secure, and thus a major source of their stress is reduced. Thus, there are both primary medication effects (on target symptoms) and secondary effects that derive from more stable interpersonal relationships.

It is clear that no magic pill can cure deep characterological wounds, but targeted medication treatment of borderline patients can be an important adjunct to psychotherapy and crisis management.

Table 10.1. Medications for Treating Borderline Subtypes

Borderline Subtype	Class of Medication
Hysteroid-dysphoria [1]	Anticonvulsants, SSRIs
Schizotypal [2]	Low doses of atypical antipsychotics [3]
Angry-impulsive [4]	SSRIs, atypical antipsychotics
Co-morbid major depression	Antidepressants [5]
Co-morbid panic disorder	Antidepressants [6]

[1] Cowdry and Gardner 1988; Liebowitz and Klein 1981; Townsend et al. 2001

[2] Soloff et al. 1986; Frances and Soloff 1988; Goldberg et al. 1986; Rocca et al. 2002; Coccaro 1998

[3] E.g., risperidone, 2 mg./day

[4] Norden 1989; Cornelius, et al. 1991; Markovitz et al. 1991; Salzman et al. 1995; Stein et al. 2000; Bogenschutz and Nurenberg 2004

[5] Except bupropion

[6] Except bupropion

Note: A study by Markovitz, et. al. (1991) suggested that adequate behavioral control with moderate-to-severe BPD clients required high doses of fluoxetine (80 mg. per day). Salzman, et. al. (1995) found that fluoxetine at lower doses (40 mg. per day) may be adequate for treating mild to moderate BPD; however, it must be noted that this dosing is higher than that generally used to treat major depression (i.e., 20 mg. per day).

The clinician should first identify which particular target symptoms are to be the focus of medication treatment. Then, before initiating treatment, also anticipate likely psychological dynamics that may be evoked around the issue of pharmacological treatment. Some potential dynamics are listed below:

- Taking medications may contribute to primitive, magical thinking, e.g., that being "fed" with pills will somehow miraculously fill up the client's inner sense of emptiness.

- Taking pills may encourage passivity.

- Recommending pharmacologic treatment may be perceived by the patient as an assault on their self. They may conclude that the therapist only sees them as a patient with a biochemical disorder.

- Drugs can be used in suicide attempts not only as a means of killing oneself but also as a way to deliver a message: "See? I killed myself with the medicines you gave me!", expressing anger towards the therapist.

- Noncompliance can be a significant issue, as it can draw the therapist into a role of monitoring the client and, in a sense, telling them what to do. This is not necessarily bad, but it can influence the interpersonal dynamics between patient and treater.

Cautions

The following four cautions are important to note:

- Treatment with anti-anxiety medications (benzodiazepines, e.g. Xanax, Klonopin, Valium, etc.) is risky with borderline patients. These patients are certainly at risk for tranquilizer abuse. In addition, clinical experience, as well as research, shows that benzodiazepines can contribute to emotional dyscontrol and increased suicidality with borderline patients (Cowdry and Gardner 1988).

- Since some borderline patients are at risk for transient psychosis, the antidepressant bupropion (a dopamine agonist) should be used with caution. This drug, which is an effective antidepressant, may precipitate psychosis in prepsychotic individuals.

- Anticonvulsants (e.g., divalproex) have mood stabilizing properties and have demonstrated effectiveness in clinical studies. However, these medications have very significant side effects and clearly are not "feel-good" drugs. Thus, in clinical practice they often fail to work effectively because of noncompliance.

- Because this group as a whole engages in frequent suicidal acting out, it is advisable to treat borderline patients with medications that have been found to have a low degree of toxicity when taken in overdose. These include antipsychotics and the following antidepressants: SSRIs, Remeron, Wellbutrin, trazodone, Cymbalta, and Effexor. Other antidepressants (e.g., tricyclics and MAO inhibitors) are quite toxic when taken in overdose and should be avoided.

Is There Something Fishy Going on Here?

Zanarini and colleagues published an amazing study exploring the use of omega-3 fatty acids (2003). This was a prospective, randomized, double-blind, placebo-controlled study. The study included thirty women diagnosed with borderline personality disorder. The treatment group received a dose of omega-3 fatty acids: one gram per day. The other group received placebo. By the end of the eight-week study the experimental group showed significant improvement in ratings of aggression and depression compared to the placebo group. Omega-3 fatty acids have been used experimentally to treat unipolar depression and bipolar disorder and may play a role in enhancing affect control. Omega-3 is found in fish oils supplements, which can be obtained at health food stores. This treatment was well tolerated, with virtually no side effects. Obviously this promising study needs to be replicated. Stay tuned!

Length of Treatment

It is unclear how long successful medication treatment should last. For some individuals many years of treatment may be indicated.

CHAPTER 11

When You Have Time for Longer-Term Therapy

Gabbard (1995) reports that about two-thirds of borderline patients drop out during the first six months of therapy. Often this occurs as the initial, more superficial relationship starts to become more meaningful to the client. Some decreases in distress coupled with fears of increasing closeness may motivate discontinuation. Conversely, many authors have noted that a significant number of borderline clients come to therapy not seeking personality growth or change, but rather searching for a long-term supportive, nurturing relationship. If ongoing therapy is available, they may become therapeutic "lifers" (Wallerstein 1986).

Sometimes this occurs as the therapist and client collude in creating an infantilizing or regressive, dependent relationship. This can contribute to stunted growth and ongoing suffering. However, it is very important to note that some patients are so profoundly wounded and incapacitated that very long-term supportive treatment is absolutely appropriate. This is what I refer to as providing "psychological dialysis." For certain people, it is a necessary, legitimate, and possibly life-sustaining treatment.

In the realm of severe personality disorders, there is considerable variability with regard to severity of the pathology and amenability to treatment. In a perfect world, clinicians would make treatment decisions based on clinical needs, which obviously differ from patient to patient. Today, however, clients and therapists alike must contend with another factor: limitations on treatment dictated by third-party payers and other agencies of managed care. While I strongly urge all therapists to lobby for appropriate treatment, we must simultaneously do our best with what we have.

I would like to suggest the following grouping of borderline clients and how these groups might be approached given the current managed care climate.

1. One-to-three sessions: This may be appropriate for three groups of patients. The first are those people who are terrified of interpersonal contact and seek out treatment only as a result of acute decompensation or are involuntarily entered into treatment (e.g., very aloof, schizoid patients). A second group would be those who (by history) have been prone to extreme regression when subject to separation stresses. As noted earlier, it may be more realistic and humane to see them only for crisis intervention, since it may well prove to be traumatic for them to enter brief therapy, become attached to the therapist, and then have to stop after ten or fifteen sessions. Finally, the last group is composed of those patients who are seen for a session or two primarily for the purpose of evaluation (e.g., to evaluate for possible hospitalization or in order to offer pharmacologic treatment recommendations to their primary care physician).

2. One-to-ten sessions: In general, the only realistic goals for this version of brief therapy are (a) to treat co-morbid Axis I disorders with psychotropic medications and/or (b) to work towards improved affective control and specific problem solving centered on a focal life problem or event. Also, it is often helpful to use this time to encourage the client to enter a support group or to begin treatment for substance abuse.

3. Twenty-to-forty sessions: Many of the approaches presented in this book are appropriate for use in conducting this rather standard version of shorter-term therapy. For many clients such treatment can be very helpful in reaching the goals outlined in Chapter 4.

4. One-to-two years of weekly therapy: This is an ideal number of sessions that can allow us to expand treatment goals. However, most managed care companies are reluctant to approve this number of sessions, despite the fact that research evidence exists to indicate that this kind of treatment is cost-effective. (See Chapter 12.)

So, let's say we have been successful in securing more visits, or we offer reduced fees,[1] or our client takes a second job to pay for therapy. (Several of my clients have done this!) What may be possible if we can work with these people for several years? We'll explore these possibilities in the next section.

_____

[1] Some authors have argued that reducing fees may constitute a form of transference gratification or a breech in the therapeutic frame. In my opinion, it all depends. In some instances to reduce fees is not helpful. It may promote regression and compromise the frame. However, some borderline people, due to their serious psychopathology, are genuinely unable to earn a decent or stable income. For these people, lowering the fee may be a humane thing to do and can be seen as a way to acknowledge a legitimate need (providing that it does not ultimately lead to the therapist feeling resentment). The astute clinician does not follow therapy guidelines rigidly, but rather is constantly assessing the *meaning of and likely consequences of* any intervention.

CHARACTEROLOGICAL CHANGE: MISSION IMPOSSIBLE?

If *fundamental* changes in the self are to occur in therapy, many would agree that very long-term treatment is necessary. Most of the literature addressing such treatment has been written by those espousing psychodynamic models. Intensive, analytically oriented psychotherapy generally requires at least two sessions per week and often lasts for a number of years (Kernberg 1975). However, an alternative model that may be realistic for some borderline clients is once-a-week therapy extending for one-to-three years. This approach can best be seen as a type of stabilizing, ego-supportive treatment such as that addressed in this book. In addition, the extra time allows us to shoot for loftier goals that may include some modifications in character structure; i.e., a type of change that psychologist Steven Johnson has referred to as a "hard-work miracle" (1985).

Beyond the goals outlined earlier in this book, two particular aspects of character change may be possible with this extended type of treatment.

The first is a modification in the client's introjects. When the therapist has been able to pass many difficult "tests," when over a lengthy period of time he/she has demonstrated consistency and reliability, and when after numerous episodes of intense emotional upheaval, the therapist has proved trustworthy and safe, something important often happens. The change likely involves a type of identification with the therapist. In particular, it becomes evident in comments made by the client that will reveal a new, less harsh, and significantly more compassionate attitude towards the self. In a sense it is as if the punitive, critical parent mode (see Chapter 1) has been silenced or, at least, the volume has been turned down. Demands on the self become more realistic, less harsh, and there is an increased capacity to accept personal limitations and to forgive oneself.

I have seen this on numerous occasions; with borderline clients it almost always takes at least a year of weekly treatment. Clients exhibit a greater ability to be decent to themselves. Their needs and feelings are now seen as more legitimate and are more genuinely acknowledged and honored. There is a greater capacity for self-empathy.

Freud spoke of "after education," which was seen as a process in which the superego is modified during psychotherapy. New, internal moral standards are adopted resulting in a decrease of harsh self-criticism. Behaviorists are more inclined to understand this as a process of social learning and modeling. Regardless of the particular theoretical explanation, it is a commonly observed phenomenon, and whether it occurs or not seems to depend on the quality of the therapeutic relationship.

The therapist must be solid, honest, trustworthy, and nonreactive. He/she must maintain the frame, hold a tight reign on countertransference, and be able to endure affective storms. Beyond this, I believe that the therapist must feel a deep and genuine care for his/her client. Borderline people have been terribly abused, neglected, and hated by important others. After a period of time (six months to a year) they are very likely to start sensing the truth of how the therapist feels, and when it is clear to them that someone genuinely does gives a damn about them, this more than anything else, sets the stage for openness to identification and new introjects.[2] Such changes in internal attitudes and self-talk may stay with the person long after treatment and serve as an ongoing inner source of self-support.

The second area for characterological change involves the modification of core schemas. Schemas are powerful and enduring beliefs, attitudes, and themes that are generally assumed to develop early in life. Initially, schemas are influenced by the multitude of interactions with important others that take place day-in and day-out over the years of early childhood. The infant comes into the world and encounters others (mainly parents and siblings). Out of his/her daily experiences, the child begins to construct basic views of the world (especially "How I am treated by others"). In circumstances where the predominant experience is that of being valued, cared for, and loved, those children probably come to see others as a source of warmth and comfort. In other settings, the experience is, of course, markedly different; too many kids encounter abuse, harshness, or neglect.

Basic schemas (or core beliefs) develop naturally out of a myriad of early experiences and tend to center around important thematic areas. This has been elaborately described by Jeffrey Young. He describes eighteen common core schemas (see appendix C).

In a sense, the particular core schemas for each person can be seen as the Achilles heels or areas of special emotional vulnerability. Thus, a person dominated by a defectiveness/unlovability schema will likely be very sensitive to life experiences that touch on this issue (while being somewhat less sensitive to events that evoke other schemas, e.g., mistrust). The theory holds that more harsh or extreme early life circumstances play a role in developing core schemas that are (1) more pronounced and (2) less malleable. This last point deserves some elaboration.

One marker of psychological health vs. psychopathology is the degree to which later life experiences are able to modify underlying schemas. People with neurotic-level character problems are certainly burdened by underlying maladaptive schemas. However, to a greater-or-lesser degree, they may be able to modify these inner beliefs when they encounter healthier, more positive, and nurturing relationships later in life (e.g., a positive, intimate relationship with a spouse, a healing experience with a mentor, or the experience of successful psychotherapy).

However, a marker of a more severe pathology is the rigidity of schemas. Even in the face of positive, "corrective experiences," underlying schemas may remain unaltered. This probably is due to at least two factors. The first is the persistence of cognitive distortions and the second takes place in the area of interpersonal relationships.

---

[2] Some authors have seen this process as a type of *re-parenting*. I think that we, as therapists, must humbly acknowledge our limitations. In so many ways true re-parenting is not possible. Many borderline people will feel better and cope more successfully, but will continue to feel intense pangs of neediness and emptiness (despite positive experiences in therapy). This not only speaks to the limitations of psychotherapy, but also to the tremendous impact (for better or for worse) of early parent-child interactions.

Let's consider an example of the persistence of cognitive distortions (obviously, this is grossly oversimplified):

Mr. Neurotic:

Core Schema:	"I am a loser . . . People hate me."
New Experience	Someone is genuinely kind to him.
Schema Modification:	"Well, maybe I'm not completely defective . . . maybe some people can like me."

Mr. Borderline:

Core Schema:	"I am a loser . . . "People hate me."
New Experience:	Someone is genuinely kind to him.
Schema Modification:	None. Inner self-talk: "They are just bull-shitting me. They really don't care." Or "Well, they might be nice to me now, but wait till they really get to know me. Then they will hate me." The new experience has failed to modify underlying beliefs, largely because Mr. Borderline has jumped to an arbitrary conclusion; in the here and now, his inner self-talk has influenced ongoing perceptions such that they serve to perpetuate existing beliefs.

The second factor contributing to the maintenance of maladaptive schemas takes place in the interpersonal arena. For example, consider what takes place when a borderline client named Simon enters a post office to purchase stamps. He is so prone to expect anger, rejection, and rebuff from others that he automatically scowls at the postal clerk, and his request for stamps is curt and abrupt, with an angry edge to his voice. The clerk backs off a bit and seems to become somewhat defensive and irritated. Simon leaves the post office thinking for the millionth time, "That jerk is just like everyone else...he hates me." Of course, it was Simon's own behavior that provoked the clerk's response. The schema is not only unmodified, it is actually strengthened. This involves not just distorted perceptions, but also *actual* interpersonal experience.

Longer-term therapy may be able to put a dent in these entrenched schemas. As described above, therapists, by repeatedly passing tests, remaining available, and genuinely caring for clients may be able to gradually modify some aspects of these underlying schemas. The reality of a non-hurtful relationship with the therapist gradually sinks in. In addition, some cognitive techniques have been suggested that aim to alter even very entrenched schemas (Young 1996).

As the therapist hears certain comments or makes inquiries about inner self-talk, the operation of underlying schemas becomes apparent. "I'm such a God-damned jerk," "I can't do anything to help myself...everything I do goes wrong." "Absolutely no one cares about whether I live or die." These statements are almost never 100 percent accurate (although they may have been that when our clients were young and living with their families of origin). Young states that by repeatedly asking the client, "Is what you said completely accurate in your life now?" the person is encouraged to challenge his/her conclusions. Repeated questioning and more accurate reality testing may gradually wear away or erode maladaptive schemas. The client cannot simply be told the more accurate perception, but must be encouraged to do the critical thinking and reality testing for himself/herself. Self-generated conclusions are more convincing. Obviously, this is neither an easy nor a quick process. It must be done over and over again, in many contexts, for it to effectively modify core schemas. I suspect that beyond a strictly cognitive level something important is also happening in the therapeutic relationship. As the therapist persistently challenges distortions and encourages reflection, the tacit messages from the therapist may be perceived as "I don't hate you" . . . "I don't think you are disgusting". . . "I think your feelings do matter" . . . or "I do have confidence that you can stand on your own two feet."

In the eyes of those who direct managed care insurance programs, such changes may not constitute "medical necessity," but they certainly can make a tremendous difference in our clients' lives.

CHAPTER 12

Psychotherapy: Terminable and Interminable

Termination rightly should be based on clinical judgment, although, unfortunately, these days limited health care benefits may be the determining factor. If the number of sessions is rigidly prescribed by third-party payers, it is very important to make it clear from the beginning of therapy, when the sessions will end. Additionally, it is a good idea to remind the client periodically of how many sessions are left. Since borderline people are often so sensitive to loss and abandonment, addressing termination issues throughout treatment helps the BPD client (1) not become too attached and (2) to prepare for the eventual end of treatment.

It should go without saying that termination issues are intimately woven together with the specific and realistic goals of therapy. I have often said to patients, "You and I both know that you can't solve all your problems in twenty sessions . . . however, we need to work hard to make the most of our time together, and I think it's realistic that you can benefit from brief therapy." Recall, the goal is not "cure," but rather to facilitate more effective coping.

Often, clients will make comments regarding termination that may reveal their worries or concerns, e.g., "What am I going to do after therapy ends?" These are legitimate issues that we need to address. Reviewing the treatment goals and making a point to highlight gains they have made can be helpful in reducing some anxiety. Beyond this, other steps may be necessary. One of the more important matters to address is to help clients take action to develop or strengthen their support system, outside of therapy. This can include active problem solving (e.g., discussing specific ways to become more involved in social and recreational activities, learning to be more asser-tive about calling or approaching friends and relatives, looking at ways the client inad-vertently isolates himself/herself, etc.). In addition, many borderline people can benefit greatly from involvement in self-help or support groups (e.g., Alcoholics Anonymous, Al-Anon, Emotions Anonymous, etc.). Sometimes it becomes necessary to strongly push clients to try out one of these groups, hopefully before psychotherapy comes to an end.

In some settings it may be possible and entirely reasonable for BPD clients to continue being seen for medication visits, if psychotropic medications have been a part of their treatment. Finally, many BPD patients ultimately are seen again for a second or third round of brief therapy (what some refer to as "serial-brief-therapy"). Generally this is offered in the event that the client encounters very significant life stressors down the road.

Beyond the steps outlined above, one additional issue is important to note. So many times borderline people have never been able to or allowed to express certain emotions (especially more tender emotions). Termination often evokes feelings of loss and sadness; also feelings of gratitude towards the therapist. A formal termination provides an excellent opportunity to encourage the open expression of these feelings and to further help the client learn ways to accept and face pain, to share emotions, and to say good-bye. Often this is also an opportunity for a degree of self-disclosure. This might include telling the client what it has meant to you to help him or her. When sincere and if shared in an appropriate way, this can be a meaningful and touch-ing experience that may be a rare event in the lives of borderline clients.

WHEN "BRIEF" AIN'T ENOUGH

For the purpose of comparison, let's consider this fact: Insurance companies and HMOs authorize liver transplants at a cost of $250,000 per procedure. The three-year survival rate for liver transplants is 20 percent (Gabbard 1996b). Yet, typically, psychiatric ben-efits are extremely limited, even given new laws, and never approach the quarter-million dollar amount. Similarly, one never hears about treatment of chronic illnesses, such as diabetes, being limited to a maximum of twelve doctor visits. Clearly, this is an absurd notion. However, it is commonplace to severely limit psychiatric treatment.

Psychiatric disorders not only cause tremendous personal suffering, they also cause significant disability. (More days are lost due to psychiatric disability than to back pain, heart disease, hypertension, or diabetes and result in considerable cost to our economy in terms of absenteeism, decreased work productivity, and increased med-ical health care costs.) For example, the cost to the U.S. economy each year due to de-pressive disorders alone is estimated at $44 billion (Greenberg, et. al. 1993).

Many psychiatric disorders, including BPD, ultimately result in suicides (10 per-cent lifetime mortality from suicide in the category of major depression, 5-10 percent in the BPD category). Some of the people who make health care decisions tend to view psychiatric disorders simply as "problems in living." For a number of our clients, this is not the case. Their disorders are quite frankly life-threatening. Some people need a wake-up call.

Good luck using arguments for "clinical necessity" and pleas for extra treatment based on humanitarian concerns. Often, it comes down to economic factors to persuade managed care insurance companies to allow extra sessions. There is a small but growing body of research that demonstrates how longer-term treatment actually can reduce health care costs (and a few managed-care companies are beginning to realize this). Let's consider the following data:

Linehan and colleagues (Heard 1994) conducted a randomized, controlled trial of DBT*; dialectical behavior therapy (with patients in this group receiving once-weekly individual therapy, and once-weekly group treatment). This was compared to a control group (which received "treatment as usual" in the community). After receiving treatment, significant differences were noted when the two groups were compared.

	DBT Group	Control Group
■ Psychiatric hospital days per year	8.5	38.8
■ Acts of self-mutilation/year	1.5	9.0

The overall savings for the DBT group after treatment was $10,000 per patient per year. The bottom line appears to be that if we pay for adequate outpatient treatment we ultimately save money. One day of psychiatric hospitalization costs about the same as eight sessions of outpatient treatment. Furthermore, hospital care for suicide attempts is extremely costly. Measures that promote cost effectiveness must begin to take overall health care utilization into consideration (Heard 1994).

In another study, Stevenson and Meares (1992) looked at a group of thirty borderline patients, and evaluated the cost-effectiveness of twice-a-week dynamic psychotherapy. The group served as its own control by assessing health care utilization for two time periods; the twelve months prior to treatment and the twelve months after receiving one year of treatment. These authors documented that the outpatient therapy was able to reduce inpatient hospitalization days by 50 percent per year and reduce outpatient medical visits by 85 percent (also see: Linehan, et al. 1991).

Beyond these economic factors, of course, are the concerns about the plight of borderline patients—chronic suffering and high rates of suicide. But let's be realistic, managed care is largely concerned with cost containment. So why the restrictions on treatment in light of the studies mentioned above? The old axiom "penny-wise, pound foolish" comes to mind. As a profession we must support and encourage studies of cost-effectiveness, and as individuals we must take a stand as advocates for our clients. One of the best uses of our clinical skills may be when we use them to help persuade managed care insurance companies to provide more visits.

---

* Dialectical behavior therapy is a specifically designed, behaviorally oriented treatment developed by psychologist Marsha Linehan.

I want to make it abundantly clear. Even though I believe we can offer a great deal to these clients in the context of shorter-term therapy, I also believe strongly that we must not compromise treatment standards. Psychotherapists from all professional disciplines must become advocates for clients, who (due to no fault of their own) have disorders that are not adequately addressed by brief psychotherapy. This is a time for unity among professionals, not division. Together, we have our best shot at influencing health care policies. Together, we can speak out and we can make a difference.

PSYCHOTHERAPY EPILOG

There are three difficult, overarching tasks for therapists who treat borderline patients. The first is to maintain a genuinely caring and respectful attitude towards patients who often are very hard to be with. We end up enduring intense emotional storms, we hear about how they can often be insensitive, hurtful, and cruel to others. Many times we become the target for angry or devaluating comments. All therapists treating borderline patients will occasionally feel worn out and completely drained after sessions. This is hard work, and yet, ultimately, our ability to hang in there with these patients can make a real difference.

The second challenge is to maintain realistic hope. This is hard to do when you hear your clients' ongoing comments reflecting extreme pessimism, or when you must witness continued suffering balanced by only minimal gains and successes. Longitudinal studies do show that a majority of BPD patients improve significantly when they reach their forties. One aspiration for therapy is to sustain them until things simmer down later in life. Psychologist Michael Mahoney refers to psychotherapists as "Guardians of hope" (1994). It's with these folks that we will experience some of our greatest challenges to this role of guardian.

Finally, there is a dialectical stance that may be necessary in treating borderline patients. This involves the ability to appreciate that on some levels, borderline people are like two-year-old children. We must have a realistic understanding of their deficiencies and limitations. However, we also must simultaneously treat them as capable adults, holding them responsible for certain actions (e.g., coming to scheduled sessions, paying fees, and, ultimately, living their lives in a responsible way) and transmitting to them our belief and confidence that they will eventually be able to stand on their own two feet.

Margaret Mead once said, "Never doubt that a small group of thoughtful, committed citizens can change the world. Indeed, it is the only thing that ever has." The work we do with our borderline clients may not seem as grand as changing the world, but it can be the kind of experience that can make a world of difference for these very wounded people. I sincerely hope that you have found this book to be helpful as you and I both continue to try to make a difference.

APPENDIX A

Assessing Borderline Personality Disorders with Psychological Tests

In most cases the diagnosis of borderline personality disorder can be made based on the patient's clinical history and current symptomatic presentation. Generally, psychological testing is not necessary in order to establish the diagnosis. Two notable exceptions are first, when the clinician suspects possible underlying borderline pathology in an individual who appears to have, at least superficially, a higher level of functioning (i.e. a primitive, borderline core with a veneer of competency and higher functioning, as described in chapter 1), or second, if there is complex co-morbidity.

Described below are several psychological instruments (self-report, structured interviews, and tests) that may be useful in establishing the diagnosis, especially in those where there may be less-than-obvious signs of borderline pathology or for whom there is complex co-morbidity.

DIAGNOSTIC INTERVIEW FOR BORDERLINE PERSONALITY DISORDERS: REVISED

This structured-interview instrument is derived from DSM criteria and exhibits a high degree of sensitivity and specificity in diagnosing BPD and in differentiating it from other personality disorders (Zanarini, et al. 1989).

BORDERLINE PERSONALITY INTERVIEW

This self-report measure is derived both from DSM criteria and from psychodynamic concepts regarding BPD. It has demonstrated reliability and validity in diagnosing BPD (Leichenring 1999). In addition, it provides information regarding reality testing, fears of closeness, and other relevant dimensions of personality functioning.

STRUCTURED CLINICAL INTERVIEW FOR DSM-III-R PERSONALITY DISORDERS (SCID-II)

The SCID was developed as a structured-interview measure for diagnosing DSM Axis I and II disorders, and it has well-established reliability and validity (Spitzer, et al. 1987).

RORSCHACH INKBLOT TECHNIQUE (EXNER'S COMPREHENSIVE SYSTEM)

In many respects, this is the ideal psychological test for assessing possible borderline pathology. Specific Rorschach indices of borderline personality disorder include:

➢ Impaired thought processes

1. Fabulized combinations and INCOMs: Smith (in Kwawer, et al., 1980, p. 66–68) indicates that this is a frequent finding among borderline patients, even in high-level BPD. Borderline individuals, however, rarely give CONTAM responses, which are more suggestive of psychotic disorders

2. Intrusions of primary process thinking may be evident in content that is primitive and morbid such as "dripping blood," "infected vagina."

➢ Egocentric and infantile level of development

1. Scores above 0.46 on the egocentricity index

2. TF and pure T responses (reflecting infantile dependency longings)

> Polarization of experiences and splitting

1. Single figure is polarized, e.g., "A man with one evil side and one good side" (Kwawer, et al. 1980, p. 260)

2. Polarized contents: e.g., "angels and devils"

> Blurred self-other perceptions

1. Amorphous and diffuse percepts: e.g., vague (v) responses

2. Symbiotic images: e.g., "two people stuck together," "a baby still attached to the umbilical cord," "Siamese twins"

3. Symbiosis themes also suggesting violence or ambivalence: e.g., Card VII: (upside down) "two women stuck together at the head with a stick of dynamite glued between the heads" or "a baby with an 'ambivical' cord"

4. Engulfment: e.g., "two amoebas swallowing each other up"

5. Separation responses: e.g., Card IV "a giant ripping himself in half"

6. Weak or permeable boundaries: e.g., Card I: "two women so close that they share the same body but have two heads"; "very fluid . . . like a jellyfish . . . you can see right through it"

> Impaired reality testing

1. Higher level BPD may have X+% in the lower end of the normal range but may exhibit one or two F– responses

2. Lower level BPD: X+%: 50–65%

> Poor affective regulation

1. FC< CF+C

2. Color shading and/or pure color responses

3. Lambda below 0.32

4. Afr: above 0.85

5. Highly affectively charged responses

MMPI-2 AND MCMI-II

These commonly used psychometric instruments are generally not helpful in making a diagnosis of BPD, lacking sensitivity and specificity for making this particular diagnosis.

Pleasant Events Checklist

This checklist is designed to find out about the things you enjoy, and to give you new ideas about pleasant things to do. The checklist contains a list of events and activities, not all of which will appeal to you (what is pleasant to one person may be torture to another!).

- ☐ Being in the country
- ☐ Wearing expensive or formal clothes
- ☐ Making contributions to religious, charitable, or other groups
- ☐ Talking about sports
- ☐ Meeting someone new of the same sex
- ☐ Taking tests when well-prepared
- ☐ Going to a rock concert
- ☐ Playing baseball or softball
- ☐ Planning trips or vacations
- ☐ Buying things for myself
- ☐ Being at the beach
- ☐ Doing artwork (painting, sculpture, drawing, movie-making, etc.)
- ☐ Rock climbing or mountaineering
- ☐ Reading the Scriptures or other sacred works
- ☐ Playing golf
- ☐ Re-arranging or redecorating my room or house
- ☐ Going naked
- ☐ Going to a sports event
- ☐ Reading a "How To Do It" book or article
- ☐ Going to the races (horse, car, boat, etc.)
- ☐ Reading stories, novels, poems, or plays
- ☐ Going to a bar, tavern, club, etc.
- ☐ Going to lectures of hearing speakers
- ☐ Driving skillfully
- ☐ Breathing clean air
- ☐ Thinking up or arranging songs or music
- ☐ Saying something clearly
- ☐ Boating (canoeing, kayaking, motorboating, sailing, etc.)
- ☐ Pleasing my parents
- ☐ Restoring antiques, refinishing furniture, etc.
- ☐ Watching TV
- ☐ Talking to myself
- ☐ Camping
- ☐ Working in politics
- ☐ Working on machines (cars, bikes, motorcycles, tractors, etc.)
- ☐ Thinking about something good in the future
- ☐ Playing cards
- ☐ Completing a difficult task

☐ Laughing
☐ Solving a problem, puzzle, crossword, etc.
☐ Being at weddings, baptisms, confirmations, etc.
☐ Criticizing someone
☐ Shaving
☐ Having lunch with friends or associates
☐ Playing tennis
☐ Taking a shower
☐ Driving long distances
☐ Woodworking, carpentry
☐ Writing stories, novels, plays, or poetry
☐ Being with animals
☐ Riding in an airplane
☐ Exploring (hiking away from known routes, spelunking, etc.)
☐ Having a frank and open conversation
☐ Singing in a group
☐ Thinking about myself or my problems
☐ Working on my job
☐ Going to a party
☐ Going to church functions (socials, classes, bazaars, etc.)
☐ Speaking a foreign language
☐ Going to service, civic, or social club meetings
☐ Going to a business meeting or convention
☐ Being in a sporty or expensive car
☐ Playing a musical instrument
☐ Making snacks
☐ Snow skiing
☐ Being helped
☐ Wearing informal clothes
☐ Combing or brushing my hair
☐ Acting
☐ Taking a nap
☐ Being with friends
☐ Canning, freezing, making preserves, etc.
☐ Driving fast
☐ Solving a personal problem
☐ Being in a city
☐ Taking a bath
☐ Singing to myself
☐ Making food or crafts to sell or give away
☐ Playing pool or billiards
☐ Being with my children or grandchildren
☐ Playing chess or checkers
☐ Doing craft work (pottery, jewelry, leather, beads, weaving, etc.)
☐ Weighing myself
☐ Scratching myself
☐ Putting on make-up, fixing my hair, etc.

☐ Designing or drafting
☐ Visiting people who are sick, shut in, or in trouble
☐ Cheering, rooting
☐ Bowling
☐ Being popular at a gathering
☐ Watching wild animals
☐ Having an original idea
☐ Gardening, landscaping, or doing yard work
☐ Going shopping
☐ Reading essays or technical, academic, or professional literature
☐ Wearing new clothes
☐ Dancing
☐ Sitting in the sun
☐ Riding a motorcycle
☐ Just sitting and thinking
☐ Seeing good things happen to my family or friends
☐ Going to a fair, carnival, circus, zoo, or amusement park
☐ Talking about philosophy or religion
☐ Gambling
☐ Planning or organizing something
☐ Having a drink by myself
☐ Listening to the sounds of nature
☐ Dating, courting, etc.
☐ Having a lively talk
☐ Racing in a car, motorcycle, boat, etc.
☐ Listening to the radio
☐ Having friends come to visit
☐ Playing in a sporting competition
☐ Introducing people who I think would like each other
☐ Giving gifts
☐ Going to school or government meetings, court sessions, etc.
☐ Getting massages or backrubs
☐ Getting letters, cards, or notes
☐ Watching the sky, clouds, or a storm
☐ Going on outings (to the park, a picnic, or a barbecue, etc.)
☐ Playing basketball
☐ Buying something for my family
☐ Photography
☐ Giving a speech or lecture
☐ Reading maps
☐ Gathering natural objects (wild foods or fruit, rocks, driftwood, etc.)
☐ Working on my finances
☐ Wearing clean clothes

- [ ] Making a major purchase or investment (car, appliance, house, stocks, etc.)
- [ ] Helping someone
- [ ] Being in the mountains
- [ ] Getting a job advancement (being promoted, getting a raise or a better job, being accepted into a better school, etc.)
- [ ] Hearing jokes
- [ ] Winning a bet
- [ ] Talking about my children or grandchildren
- [ ] Meeting someone new of the opposite sex
- [ ] Going to a revival meeting or crusade
- [ ] Talking about my health
- [ ] Seeing beautiful scenery
- [ ] Eating good meals
- [ ] Improving my health (having my teeth fixed, getting new glasses, changing my diet, etc.)
- [ ] Being downtown
- [ ] Wrestling or boxing
- [ ] Hunting or shooting
- [ ] Playing in a musical group
- [ ] Hiking
- [ ] Going to a museum or exhibit
- [ ] Writing papers, essays, articles, reports, memos, etc.
- [ ] Doing a job well
- [ ] Having spare time
- [ ] Fishing
- [ ] Loaning something
- [ ] Being noticed as sexually attractive
- [ ] Pleasing employers, teachers, etc.
- [ ] Counseling someone
- [ ] Going to a health club, sauna bath, etc.
- [ ] Having someone give me constructive feedback
- [ ] Learning to do something new
- [ ] Going to a "Drive-in" (Dairy Queen, McDonald's, etc.)
- [ ] Complimenting or praising someone
- [ ] Thinking about people I like
- [ ] Being at a fraternity or sorority
- [ ] Being with my parents
- [ ] Horseback riding
- [ ] Protesting social, political, or environmental conditions
- [ ] Talking on the telephone
- [ ] Having daydreams
- [ ] Kicking leaves, sand, pebbles, etc.
- [ ] Playing lawn sports (badminton, croquet, shuffleboard, horseshoes, etc.)
- [ ] Going to school reunions, alumni meetings, etc.
- [ ] Seeing famous people
- [ ] Going to the movies
- [ ] Kissing
- [ ] Being alone
- [ ] Budgeting my time
- [ ] Cooking meals
- [ ] Being praised by people I admire
- [ ] Outwitting a "superior"
- [ ] Feeling the presence of the Lord in my life
- [ ] Doing a project in my own way
- [ ] Doing odd jobs around the house
- [ ] Having a good cry
- [ ] Being at a family reunion or get-together
- [ ] Giving a party or get-together
- [ ] Washing my hair
- [ ] Coaching someone
- [ ] Going to a restaurant
- [ ] Seeing or smelling a flower or plant
- [ ] Being invited out
- [ ] Receiving honors (civic, military, etc.)
- [ ] Using cologne, perfume, or aftershave
- [ ] Having someone agree with me
- [ ] Reminiscing, talking about old times
- [ ] Getting up early in the morning
- [ ] Having peace and quiet
- [ ] Doing experiments or other scientific work
- [ ] Visiting friends
- [ ] Writing in a diary
- [ ] Playing football
- [ ] Being counseled
- [ ] Saying prayers
- [ ] Giving massages or backrubs
- [ ] Hitchhiking
- [ ] Meditating or doing yoga
- [ ] Doing favors for people
- [ ] Talking with people on the job or in class
- [ ] Being relaxed
- [ ] Being asked for my help or advice
- [ ] Thinking about other people's problems
- [ ] Playing board games (Monopoly, Scrabble, etc.)
- [ ] Sleeping soundly at night
- [ ] Doing heavy outdoor work (cutting or chopping wood, clearing land, farm work, etc.)
- [ ] Reading the newspaper
- [ ] Snowmobiling or dune-buggy riding
- [ ] Being in a body-awareness, sensitivity, encounter, therapy, or "rap" group
- [ ] Dreaming at night
- [ ] Playing ping pong

- ☐ Brushing my teeth
- ☐ Swimming
- ☐ Running, jogging, or doing gymnastic, fitness, or field exercises
- ☐ Walking barefoot
- ☐ Playing frisbee or catch
- ☐ Doing housework or laundry; cleaning things
- ☐ Being with my roommate
- ☐ Listening to music
- ☐ Arguing
- ☐ Knitting, crocheting, embroidery, or fancy needlework
- ☐ Petting, necking
- ☐ Amusing people
- ☐ Talking about sex
- ☐ Having houseguests
- ☐ Being with someone I love
- ☐ Reading magazines
- ☐ Sleeping late
- ☐ Starting a new project
- ☐ Being stubborn
- ☐ Having sex
- ☐ Having other sexual satisfactions
- ☐ Going to the library
- ☐ Playing soccer, rugby, hockey, lacrosse, etc.
- ☐ Preparing a new or special food
- ☐ Birdwatching
- ☐ Watching people
- ☐ Building or watching a fire
- ☐ Winning an argument
- ☐ Selling or trading something
- ☐ Finishing a project or task
- ☐ Confessing or apologizing
- ☐ Repairing things
- ☐ Working with others as a team
- ☐ Bicycling
- ☐ Telling people what to do
- ☐ Being with happy people
- ☐ Playing party games
- ☐ Writing letters, cards, or notes
- ☐ Talking about politics or public affairs
- ☐ Asking for help or advice
- ☐ Going to banquets, luncheons, potlucks, etc.
- ☐ Talking about my hobby or special interest
- ☐ Watching attractive women or men
- ☐ Smiling at people
- ☐ Playing in sand, a stream, the grass, etc.
- ☐ Talking about other people
- ☐ Being with my husband or wife
- ☐ Having people show interest in what I have said
- ☐ Going on field trips, nature walks, etc.
- ☐ Expressing my love to someone
- ☐ Caring for houseplants
- ☐ Having coffee, tea, a coke, etc., with friends
- ☐ Taking a walk
- ☐ Collecting things
- ☐ Playing handball, paddleball, squash, etc.
- ☐ Sewing
- ☐ Remembering a departed friend or loved one, visiting the cemetery
- ☐ Doing things with children
- ☐ Beachcombing
- ☐ Being complimented or told I have done well
- ☐ Being told I am loved
- ☐ Eating snacks
- ☐ Staying up late
- ☐ Having family members or friends do something that makes me proud of them
- ☐ Being with my children
- ☐ Going to auctions, garage sales, etc.
- ☐ Thinking about an interesting question
- ☐ Doing volunteer work; working on community service projects
- ☐ Water skiing, surfing, scuba diving
- ☐ Receiving money
- ☐ Defending or protecting someone; stopping fraud or abuse
- ☐ Hearing a good sermon
- ☐ Picking up a hitchhiker
- ☐ Winning a competition
- ☐ Making a new friend
- ☐ Talking about my job or school
- ☐ Reading cartoons, comic strips, or comic books
- ☐ Borrowing something
- ☐ Traveling with a group
- ☐ Seeing old friends
- ☐ Teaching someone
- ☐ Using my strength
- ☐ Traveling
- ☐ Going to office parties or departmental get-togethers
- ☐ Attending a concert, opera, or ballet
- ☐ Playing with pets
- ☐ Going to a play
- ☐ Looking at the stars or moon
- ☐ Being coached

Reprinted with permission from "The Pleasant Events Schedule: Studies on Reliability, Validity, and Scale," by D. MacPhillamy and D. M. Lewinsohn in the *Journal of Consulting and Clinical Psychology* (1982) 50:363–380.

APPENDIX C

Early Maladaptive Schemas

(Revised Schema Listing; January, 1994)*

DISCONNECTION AND REJECTION

(Expectation that one's needs for security, safety, stability, nurturance, empathy, sharing of feelings, acceptance, and respect will not be met in a predictable manner. Typical family origin is detached, explosive, unpredictable, rejecting, punitive, unforgiving, withholding, inhibited, or abusive.)

1. *Abandonment/Instability.* The perceived *instability* or *unreliability* of those available for support and connection.

   Involves the sense that significant others will not be able to continue providing emotional support, connection, strength, or practical protection because they are emotionally unstable and unpredictable (e.g., angry outbursts), unreliable, or erratically present; because they will die imminently; or because they will abandon the patient in favor of someone better.

2. *Mistrust/Abuse.* The expectation that others will hurt, abuse, humiliate, cheat, lie, manipulate, or take advantage. Usually involves the perception that the harm is intentional or the result of unjustified and extreme

* Developed by Jeffrey E. Young, Ph.D. Copyright © 1994 by the Professional Resource Exchange, Inc. and reproduced by permission. For more information, write: Cognitive Therapy Center of New York, 3 East 80th Street, Penthouse, New York, NY 10021 or telephone (212) 717-1052.

negligence. May include the sense that one always ends up being cheated relative to others or "getting the short end of the stick."

3. *Emotional Deprivation.* Expectation that one's desire for a normal degree of emotional support will not be adequately met by others. The three major forms of deprivation are:

   a. Deprivation of Nurturance—Absence of attention, affection, warmth, or companionship.

   b. Deprivation of Empathy—Absence of understanding, listening, self-disclosure, or mutual sharing of feelings from others.

   c. Deprivation of Protection—Absence of strength, direction, or guidance from others.

4. *Defectiveness/Shame.* The feeling that one is defective, bad, unwanted, inferior, or invalid in important respects; or that one would be unlovable to significant others if exposed. May involve hypersensitivity to criticism, rejection, and blame; self-consciousness, comparisons, and insecurity around others; or a sense of shame regarding one's perceived flaws. These flaws may be *internal* (e.g., selfishness, angry impulses, unacceptable sexual desires) or *external* (e.g., undesirable physical appearance, social awkwardness).

5. *Social Isolation/Alienation.* The feeling that one is isolated from the rest of the world, different from other people, and/or not part of any group or community.

IMPAIRED AUTONOMY AND PERFORMANCE

(Expectations about oneself and the environment that interfere with one's perceived ability to separate, survive, function independently, or perform successfully. Typical family origin is enmeshed, undermining of child's confidence, overprotective, or failing to reinforce child for performing competently outside the family.)

6. *Dependence/Incompetence.* Belief that one is unable to handle one's *everyday responsibilities* in a competent manner, without considerable help from others (e.g., take care of oneself, solve daily problems, exercise good judgment, tackle new tasks, make good decisions). Often presents as helplessness.

7. *Vulnerability to Danger.* Exaggerated fear that "random" catastrophe could strike at any time and that one will be unable to prevent it. Fears focus on one or more of the following: (a) *Medical*—heart attack, AIDS; (b) *Emotional*—go crazy; (c) *Natural/Phobic*—elevators, crime, airplanes, earthquakes.

8. *Enmeshment/Undeveloped Self.* Excessive emotional involvement and closeness with one or more significant others (often parents), at the expense of full

individuation or normal social development. Often involves the belief that at least one of the enmeshed individuals cannot survive or be happy without the constant support of the other. May also include feelings of being smothered by, or fused with, others or insufficient individual identity. Often experienced as a feeling of emptiness and floundering, having no direction, or in extreme cases questioning one's existence.

9. *Failure.* The belief that one has failed, will inevitably fail, or is fundamentally inadequate relative to one's peers, in areas of *achievement* (school, career, sports, etc.). Often involves beliefs that one is stupid, inept, untalented, ignorant, lower in status, less successful than others, and so on.

IMPAIRED LIMITS

(Deficiency in internal limits, responsibility to others, or long-term goal-orientation. Leads to difficulty respecting the rights of others, making commitments, or setting and meeting personal goals. Typical family origin is characterized by permissiveness, indulgence, or lack of direction, rather than appropriate confrontation, discipline, and limits in relation to taking responsibility and setting goals. Child may not have been pushed to tolerate normal levels of discomfort, or may not have been given adequate supervision, direction, or guidance.)

10. *Entitlement/Domination.* Insistence that one should be able to do or have whatever one wants, regardless of what others consider reasonable or the cost to others; or the excessive tendency to assert one's power, force one's point of view, or control the behavior of others in line with one's own desires—without regard to others' needs for autonomy and self-direction. Often involves excessive demandingness and lack of empathy for others' needs and feelings.

11. *Insufficient Self-Control/Self-Discipline.* Pervasive difficulty or refusal to exercise sufficient self-control and frustration tolerance to achieve one's personal goals, or to restrain the excessive expression of one's emotions and impulses. In its milder form, patient presents with an exaggerated emphasis on *discomfort-avoidance:* avoiding pain, conflict, confrontation, responsibility, or overexertion—at the expense of personal fulfillment, commitment, or integrity.

OTHER-DIRECTEDNESS

(An excessive focus on the desires, feelings, and responses of others, at the expense of one's own needs—in order to gain love and approval, maintain one's sense of connection, or avoid retaliation. Usually involves suppression and lack of awareness regarding one's own anger and natural inclinations. Typical family origin is based on conditional acceptance: children must suppress important aspects of themselves in order to gain love, attention, and approval. In many such families, the parents' emotional needs and desires—or social acceptance and status—are valued more than the unique needs and feelings of each child.)

12. *Subjugation.*   Excessive surrendering of control over one's behavior, emotional expression, and decisions, because one feels *coerced*—usually to avoid anger, retaliation, or abandonment. Involves the perception that one's own desires, opinions, and feelings are not valid or important to others. Frequently presents as excessive compliance, combined with hypersensitivity to feeling trapped.

  Almost always involves the chronic *suppression of anger* toward those perceived to be in control. Usually leads to a build-up of anger that is manifested in maladaptive symptoms (e.g., passive-aggressive behavior, uncontrolled outbursts of temper, psychosomatic symptoms, withdrawal of affection, "acting out," substance abuse).

13. *Self-Sacrifice.* Excessive focus on *voluntarily* meeting the needs of others in daily situations, at the expense of one's own gratification. The most common reasons are to prevent causing pain to others, to avoid guilt from feeling selfish, or to maintain the connection with others perceived as needy. Often results from an acute sensitivity to the pain of others. Sometimes leads to a sense that one's own needs are not being adequately met and to resentment of those who are taken care of. (Overlaps with concept of co-dependency.)

14. *Approval-Seeking.* Excessive emphasis on gaining approval, recognition, or attention from other people, or fitting in, at the expense of developing a secure and true sense of self. One's sense of esteem is dependent primarily on the reactions of others, rather than one's own internalized values, standards, or natural inclinations. Sometimes includes an overemphasis on status, appearance, social acceptance, money, competition, or achievement—being among the best or most popular—as means of gaining approval. Frequently results in major life decisions that are inauthentic or unsatisfying, hypersensitivity to rejection, or envy of others who are more popular or successful.

OVERVIGILANCE AND INHIBITION

(Excessive emphasis on controlling one's spontaneous feelings, impulses, and choices in order to avoid making mistakes or on meeting rigid, internalized rules and expectations about performance and ethical behavior—often at the expense of happiness, self-expression, relaxation, close relationships, or health. Typical family origin is grim [and sometimes punitive]: performance, duty, perfectionism, following rules, and avoiding costly mistakes predominate over pleasure, joy, and relaxation. There is usually an undercurrent of pessimism and worry—that things could fall apart if one fails to be vigilant and careful at all times.)

15. *Vulnerability to Error/Negativity.* Exaggerated expectation—in a wide range of work, financial, or interpersonal situations that are typically viewed as "controllable"—that things will go seriously wrong, or that aspects of one's life that seem to be going well will fall apart at any time *or* a pervasive, life-long focus on the negative aspects of life (pain, death, loss, disappointment, conflict, guilt, resentment, unsolved problems, potential mistakes, betrayal, things that could go wrong, etc.) while minimizing or neglecting the positive or optimistic aspects. Usually involves an inordinate fear of making mistakes that might lead to financial collapse, loss, humiliation, being trapped in a bad situation, or loss of control. Because potential negative outcomes are exaggerated, these patients are frequently characterized by chronic worry, vigilance, pessimism, complaining, or indecision.

16. *Overcontrol.* The excessive inhibition of spontaneous action, feeling, or communication—usually to avoid making mistakes, disapproval by others, catastrophe and chaos, or losing control of one's impulses. The most common areas of excessive control involve (a) inhibition of *anger* and aggression, (b) compulsive *order* and planning, (c) inhibition of *positive impulses* (e.g., joy, affection, sexual excitement, play), (d) excessive adherence to routine or ritual, and (e) difficulty expressing *vulnerability* or *communicating* freely about one's feelings, needs, and so forth. Often the overcontrol is extended to others in the patient's environment.

17. *Unrelenting Standards.* The underlying belief that one must strive to meet very high *internalized standards* of behavior and performance, usually to avoid criticism. Typically results in feelings of pressure or difficulty slowing down, and in hypercriticalness toward oneself and others. Must involve significant impairment in pleasure, relaxation, health, self-esteem, sense of accomplishment, or satisfying relationships.

   Unrelenting standards typically present as (a) *perfectionism,* inordinate attention to detail, and an underestimate of how good one's own performance is relative to the norm; (b) *rigid rules* or "shoulds" in many areas of life, including unrealistically high moral, ethical, cultural, or religious precepts; or (c) preoccupation with *time and efficiency,* so that more can be accomplished.

18. *Punitiveness.* The tendency to be angry, intolerant, harshly critical, punitive, and impatient with those people (including oneself) who do not meet one's expectations or standards. Usually includes difficulty forgiving mistakes or tolerating limitations in oneself or others, because of a reluctance to consider extenuating circumstances, allow for human imperfection, empathize with feelings, be flexible, or see alternative points of view.

References

American Psychiatric Association. 1994. *Diagnostic and Statistical Manual of Mental Disorders, Fourth Edition*. Washington, D. C.: American Psychiatric Association.

Andrulonis, P. A. and N. G. Vogel. 1984. "Comparison of Borderline Personality Sub-categories to Schizophrenic and Affective Disorders." *British Journal of Psychiatry* 144:358-363.

Avis, H. 1993. *Drugs and Life*. Dubuque, Iowa: W. C. Brown & Benchmark.

Beck, A. T. 1976. "*Cognitive Therapy and the Emotional Disorders*." New York: New American Library, Inc.

Bellak, L., M. Hurvich, and H. K. Gedimen. 1973. *Ego Functions in Schizophrenics, Neurotics, and Normals: A Systematic Study of Conceptual Diagnostic and Therapeutic Aspects*. New York: John Wiley and Sons.

Blanck, G. and R. Blanck. 1979. *Ego Psychology*: II. New York: Columbia University Press.

Bogenschutz, M. P. and G. H. Nurnberg. 2004. Olanzapine versus placebo in the treatment of borderline personality disorder. *Journal of Clinical Psychiatry* 65(1):104-109.

Brodsky, B. S. and J. J. Mann. 1997. "Risk Factors for Suicidal Behavior in Borderline Personality Disorder." *The Journal of the California Alliance for the Mentally Ill* 1:27-28.

Burns, D. D. 1980. *Feeling Good: The New Mood Therapy*. New York: The American Library, Inc.

Coccaro, E. F. 1998. Clinical outcome of psychopharmacologic treatment of borderline and schizotypal personality disordered subjects. *Journal of Clinical Psychiatry* 59(Suppl): 130-135.

Coleson, D., L. Lewis, and L. Horvitz. 1985. "Negative Outcome in Psychotherapy and Psychoanalysis" In *Negative Outcome in Psychotherapy and What to Do About It*, edited by D. T. May and C. M. Franks. New York: Springer.

Cornelius, J. R., P. H. Soloff, J. M. Perel, and R. F. Ulrich. 1991. "A Preliminary Trial of Fluoxetine in Refractory Borderline Patients." *Journal of Clinical Psychopharmacology*. 11: 116-120.

Cowdry, R. W. and O. L. Gardner. 1988. "Pharmacotherapy of Borderline Personality Disorder." *Archives of General Psychiatry* 45:111-119.

Deutsch, H. 1944. *The Psychology of Women*. New York: Grune & Stratton.

Essex, M. J., et al. 2002. Maternal stress beginning in infancy may sensitize children to later stress exposure: Effects on cortisol and behavior. *Biological Psychiatry* 52:776-784.

Frances, A. and P. H. Soloff. 1988. "Treating the Borderline Patient with Low-Dose Neuroleptics." *Hospital and Community Psychiatry* 39(3):246-248.

Frey, W. H, C. Hoffman-Ahern, et al. 1983. Crying behavior in the human adult. *Integrative Psychiatry* 1:94-100.

Gabbard, G. O. 1996a. "Integrated Treatment of Borderline Personality Disorder." *Psychiatric Times*, April 1996:24-27.

Gabbard, G. O. 1996b. *Cost Effectiveness of Psychotherapy*. San Francisco: CME, Inc. Conference.

Gabbard, G. O. 1995. Treatment of Borderline Personality Disorder. San Diego, CA: Talk at the U.S. Psychiatric Congress.

Gabbard, G. O., L. Horwitz, J. G. Allen, et al. 1994. "Transference Interpretation in the Psychotherapy of Borderline Patients: A High Risk, High-Gain Phenomenon." *Harvard Review of Psychiatry* 2:59-69.

Goldberg, S. C., S. C. Schulz, P. M. Schulz, R. J. Resnick, R. M. Hamer, and R. O. Friedel. 1986. "Borderline and Schizotypal Personality Disorders Treated with Low Dose Thiothixene vs. Placebo." *Archives of General Psychiatry* 43:680-686.

Greenberg, P. E., et al. 1993. "The Economic Burden of Depression in 1990." *Journal of Clinical Psychiatry* 54:405-418.

Grinker, Jr., R. R., B. Werble, and R. C Drye. 1968. *The Borderline Syndrome: A Behavioral Study of Ego-Functions*. New York: Basic Books.

Gunderson, J. 2003. *New Developments in the Treatment of Borderline Personality Disorders*. U.S. Psychiatric and Mental Health Congress, Orlando, Florida.

Gunderson, J. G. and K. A. Phillips. 1991. "A Current View of the Interface Between Borderline Personality Disorder and Depression." *American Journal of Psychiatry* 148(8):967-975.

Gunderson, J. G. and M. C. Zanarini. 1987. "Current Overview of the Borderline Diagnosis." *Journal of Clinical Psychiatry* 48(8):5-14.

Gundersen, J. G. and M. T. Singer. 1975. "Defining Borderline Patients: an Overview." *American Journal of Psychiatry* 132:1-10.

Heard, H. 1994. Behavior Therapies for Borderline Patients. Presented at the American Psychiatric Association Annual Meeting, Philadelphia.

Heim, C. and C. P. Nemeroff. 2002. Neurobiology of early life stress: Clinical studies. *Seminars in Clinical Neuropsychiatry* 7(2):147-159.

Heim, C., et al. 2000. Pituitary-adrenal and autonomic responses to stress in women after sexual and physical abuse in childhood. *JAMA* 284(5):592-597.

Herman, J. L., J. C. Perry, and B. A. van der Kolk. 1989. "Childhood Trauma in Borderline Personality Disorder." *American Journal of Psychiatry* 146:490-495.

Hoch, P. and P. Polatin. 1949. "Pseudoneurotic Forms of Schizophrenia." *Psychiatric Quarterly* 23:248-276.

Horwitz, L., G. O Gabbard, J. G. Allen, et al. 1996. *Borderline Personality Disorder: Tailoring the Psychotherapy to the Patient*. Washington, D.C.: American Psychiatric Press.

Johnson, S. M. 1985. *Characterological Transformation*. New York: W. W. Norton and Co.

Kabat-Zinn, J. 1990. *Full Catastrophe Living: Using the Wisdom of Your Body and Mind to Face Stress, Pain, and Illness*. New York: Dell.

Kemperman, I., M. J. Russ, et al. 1997. Self-injurious behavior and mood regulation in borderline patients. *Journal of Personality Disorders* 11(2):146-157.

Kernberg, O. F. 1975. *Borderline Conditions and Pathological Narcissism*. New York: Jason Aronson.

Kernberg, O. F. 1967. "Borderline Personality Organization." *Journal of the American Psychoanalytic Association* 15:641-685.

Klein, D. F. and J. M. Davis. 1969. *Diagnosis and Drug Treatment of Psychiatric Disorders*. Second Edition. Baltimore: Williams and Wilkins.

Knight, R. 1953. "Borderline States." *Bulletin of the Menninger Clinic* 17:1-12.

Kroll, J. 1988. *The Challenge of the Borderline Patient*. New York: W. W. Norton and Co.

Kwawer, J. S., H. D. Lerner, et al. 1980. *Borderline Phenomena and the Rorschach Test*. New York: International University Press, Inc.

Leibenluft, E., D. L. Gardner, and R. W. Cowdry. 1987. "The Inner Experience of the Borderline Self-Mutilator." *Journal of Personality Disorders* 1:317-324.

Leibovich, M. A. 1983. "Why Short-Term Psychotherapy for Borderlines?" *Psychother. Psychosom.* 39:1-9.

Lewis, T., et al. 2000. *A General Theory of Love*. New York: Random House.

Liebowitz, M. R. and D. F. Klein. 1981. "Interrelationships of Hysteroid-Dysphoria and Borderline Personality Disorder." *Psychiatric Clinics of North America* 4:67-87.

Leichsenrigh, F. 1999. Development and first results of the Borderline Personality Inventory: A self-report instrument for assessing borderline personality organization. *Journal of Personality Assessment* 73(1):45-63.

Linehan, M. M. 1993a. *Cognitive-Behavioral Treatment of Borderline Personality Disorder*. New York: Guilford Press.

Linehan, M. M. 1993b. *Skills Training Manual for Treating Borderline Personality Disorder*. New York: Guilford Press.

Linehan, M. M., H. E. Armstrong, et al. 1991. Cognitive-behavioral treatment of chronically parasuicidal borderline patients. *Archives of General Psychiatry* 48:1060-1064.

Mahler, M. S. and L. J Kaplan. 1977. "Developmental Aspects in the Assessment of Narcissistic and So-Called Borderline Personalities." In *Borderline Personality Disorders*, edited by P. Hartocollis. New York: International Universities Press, 71-85.

Mahler, M. S., F. Pine, and A. Bergman. 1975. *The Psychological Birth of the Human Infant: Symbiosis and Individuation*. New York: Basic Books.

Mahoney, M. J. 1991. *Human Change Process*. New York: Basic Books.

Markovitz, P. J., J. R Calabrese, S. C. Schulz, et al. 1991. "Fluoxetine in the Treatment of Borderline and Schizotypal Personality Disorders." *American Journal of Psychiatry* 148: 1064-1067.

Marmar, C. R. 1991. "Grief and Bereavement after Traumatic Loss." *Audio Digest Psychiatry* 20 (5) Glendale, CA: California Medical Association.

Masterson, J. F. 1976. *Psychotherapy of the Borderline Adult: A Developmental Approach.* New York: Brunner/Mazel.

McGlashan, T. H. 1986. "The Chestnut Lodge Follow-up Study." *Archives of General Psychiatry* 43:20-30.

Nathanson, D. L. 1992. "Shame and Compassion in Borderline Illness." *Audio Digest Psychiatry* 21(13) Glendale, CA.: Audio Digest Foundation.

Norden, M. J. 1989. "Fluoxetine in Borderline Personality Disorder." *Progress in Neuropsychopharmacological Biological Psychiatry* 13:885-893.

Peck, M. S. 1978. *The Road Less Traveled.* New York: Simon and Schuster, Inc.

Perry, J. C., J. L. Herman, et al. 1990. Psychotherapy and psychological trauma in borderline personality disorders. *Psychiatric Annals* 20(1):33-43.

Perry, J. C., et al. 1999. Effectiveness of psychotherapy for personality disorders. *American Journal of Psychiatry* 156:1312-1321.

Preston, J. D., N. Varzos, and D. Liebert. 1995. *Every Session Counts: Making the Most of Your Brief Therapy.* San Luis Obispo, CA.: Impact Publishers.

Preston, J. D., J. O'Neal, and M. Talaga. 1994. *Handbook of Clinical Psychopharmacology for Therapists.* Oakland, CA.: New Harbinger Publications.

Preston, J. D. 1993. *Growing Beyond Emotional Pain.* San Luis Obispo, CA.: Impact Publishers.

Rocca, P., L. Marchiaro, et al. 2002. Treatment of borderline personality disorder with risperidone. *Journal of Clinical Psychiatry* 63(3):241-244.

Ronningstam, E. and J. Gunderson. 1996. "Narcissistic Personality: A Stable Disorder or a State of Mind?" *Psychiatric Times*, February, 35-36.

Russ, M. J., S. D. Roth, and A. Lerman, et al. 1992. "Pain Perception in Self-Injurious Patients with Borderline Personality Disorder." *Biological Psychiatry* 32:501-511.

Salzman, C., A. N. Wolfson, A. Schatzberg, et al. 1995. "Effect of Fluoxetine on Anger in Symptomatic Volunteers with Borderline Personality Disorder." *Journal of Clinical Psychopharmacology* 15(1):23-29.

Schore, A. N. 2001. The effects of early relational trauma on right brain development, affect regulation, and infant health. *Infant Mental Health Journal* 22(1-2):201-269.

Silk, K. R., J. Goodson, J. Benjamin, and N. Lohr. 1994. "Borderline Personality Disorder and the Anxiety Disorders" In *Biological and Neurobehavioral Studies of Borderline Personality Disorder*, edited by K. R. Silk. Washington D.C.: American Psychiatric Press.

Soloff, P. H., A. George, R. S. Nathan, P. M. Schulz, R. F. Ulrich, and J. M. Perel. 1986. "Progress in Psychopharmacology of Borderline Disorders." *Archives of General Psychiatry* 43: 691-697.

Spitzer, R. L., J. B. W. Williams, and M. Gibbon. 1987. *Structured Clinical Interview for DSM-III-R.* New York: New York state Psychiatric Institute.

Stein, M. B., N. A. Kline, and J. L. Matloff. 2002. Adjunctive olanzapine for SSRI-resistant combat-related PTSD. *American Journal of Psychiatry* 159(10):1777-1779.

Stevenson, J. and R. Meares. 1992. "An Outcome Study of Psychotherapy for Patients with Borderline Personality Disorder." *American Journal of Psychiatry* 149(3):358-362.

Stone, M. H., S. W. Hurt, and D. K. Stone. 1988. "The P.I.-500: Long-Term Follow-up of Borderline Patients Meeting DSM-III Criteria; I: Global Outcome." *Journal of Personality Disorders* 1:291-298.

Stone, M. H. 1987. "Psychotherapy of Borderline Patients in Light of Long-Term Follow-up." *Bulletin of the Menninger Clinic* 51:231-247.

Stone, M. H. 1980. *The Borderline Syndrome: Constitution, Personality, and Adaptation*. New York: McGraw-Hill.

Strupp, H. H. and J. L. Binder. 1984. *Psychotherapy in a New Key*. New York: Basic Books.

Teicher, M. H., et al. 2002. Developmental neurobiology of childhood stress and trauma. *Psychiatric Clinics of North America* 25(2):397-426.

Teicher, M. H., I. Yutaka, C. A. Glod, F. Schiffer, and H. A. Gelbard. 1994. "Early Abuse, Limbic System Dysfunction and Borderline Personality Disorder" In *Biological and Neurobehavioral Studies of Borderline Personality Disorder*, edited by K. R. Silk. Washington, D.C.: American Psychiatric Press.

Townsend, M. H., K. M. Cambre, and J. G. Barber. 2001. Treatment of borderline personality disorder with mood instability with divalproex sodium. *Journal of Clinical Psychopharmacology* 21(2):249-251.

van der Kolk, B. A. 1996. "The Body Keeps the Score: Approaches to the Psychobiology of PostTraumatic Stress Disorder" In *Traumatic Stress*, edited by B. A. van der Kolk, A. C. McFarlane, and L. Weisaeth. New York: The Guilford Press, 214-241.

van der Kolk, B. A. and M. J. Greenberg. 1987. "The Psychobiology of the Trauma Response: Hyperarousal, Constriction and Addiction to Traumatic Reexposure" In *Psychological Trauma*, edited by B. A. van der Kolk. Washington, D.C.: American Psychiatric Press.

Waldinger, R. J. and J. G. Gunderson. 1987. *Effective Psychotherapy with Borderline Patients: Case Studies*. Washington, D.C.: American Psychiatric Press.

Wallerstein, R. S. 1986. *Forty-Two Lives in Treatment: A Study of Psychoanalysis and Psychotherapy*. New York: Guilford Press.

Weiss, J. M. and C. D. Kilts. 1995. "Animal Models of Depression and Schizophrenia." In *The American Psychiatric Press Textbook of Psychopharmacology*, edited by A. F. Schatzberg and C. B. Nemeroff. Washington, D.C.: American Psychiatric Press, Inc., 81-124.

Young, J. E. 1994. Cognitive Therapy for Personality Disorders: A Schema Focused Approach, Revised Edition. Sarasota, FL: Professional Resources Press.

Young, J. 1996. "Schema-Focused Therapy for Borderline Patients." *Audio Digest Psychiatry* 25 Nos. 18-19.

Zanarini, M.C. and F. R. Frankenburg. 2003. Omega-3 fatty acid treatment of women with borderline personality disorder: A double blind, placebo-controlled pilot study. *American Journal of Psychiatry* 160(1):167-169.

Zanarini, M. C. 1996. *The Role of Sexual Abuse in the Etiology of Borderline Personality Disorder*. Washington, D.C.: American Psychiatric Press.

Zanarini, M. C., J. G. Gunderson, et al. 1989. The revised diagnostic interview for borderlines: Discriminating BPD from other Axis II disorders. *Journal of Personality Disorders* 3(1):10-18

Index

John D. Preston, Psy.D., ABPP, is a licensed psychologist and the author of fourteen books. He is professor of psychology at Alliant International University and has served on the faculty of the University of California, Davis, School of Medicine. He lectures widely in the United States and abroad. He is the recipient of the Mental Health Association President's Award for contributions to the mental health professions. His publications include *The Handbook of Clinical Psychopharmacology for Therapists, Child and Adolescent Psychopharmacology Made Simple,* and *Clinical Psychopharmacology Made Ridiculously Simple*

Some Other
New Harbinger Titles